D
WYN

Warlock at the Wheel
and other stories

Also by Diana Wynne Jones

Archer's Goon
Black Maria
Castle in the Air
Charmed Life
Dogsbody
Eight Days of Luke
Fire and Hemlock
Hexwood
The Homeward Bounders
Howl's Moving Castle
The Lives of Christopher Chant
The Magicians of Caprona
A Tale of Time City
Who Got Rid of Angus Flint?
Wild Robert
Witch Week

First published 1984 by Macmillan Children's Books
Published 1989 by Beaver, an imprint of Century Hutchinson Ltd.

This edition published 1997 by Mammoth, an imprint of Reed International Books Ltd
Michelin House, 81 Fulham Road, London SW3 6RB
and Auckland, Melbourne, Singapore and Toronto

The moral right of the author has been asserted.

ISBN 0 7497 2635 0

10 9 8 7 6 5 4 3 2 1

A CIP catalogue record for this title
is available from the British Library

Printed and bound in Great Britain
by Cox & Wyman Ltd, Reading, Berkshire

This paperback is sold subject to the condition
that it shall not, by way of trade or otherwise,
be lent, resold, hired out, or otherwise circulated
without the publisher's prior consent in any form
of binding or cover other than that in which
it is published and without a similar condition
including this condition being imposed
on the subsequent purchaser.

Contents

Warlock at the Wheel	5
The Plague of Peacocks	24
The Fluffy Pink Toadstool	37
Auntie Bea's Day Out	46
Carruthers	58
No One	82
Dragon Reserve, Home Eight	111
The Sage of Theare	144

To Marnie

The Fluffy Pink Toadstool first published in Puffin Post, Vol. 13 No. 4, 1979; *Auntie Bea's Day Out* first published in THE CATFLAP AND THE APPLE PIE, W.H. Allen, 1979; *Carruthers* first published in YOUNG WINTER'S TALES 8, Macmillan London Ltd, 1978; *The Sage of Theare* first published in HECATE'S CAULDRON, Daw, 1982

This collection copyright © Diana Wynne Jones 1984
Warlock at the Wheel © Diana Wynne Jones 1984
The Plague of Peacocks © Diana Wynne Jones 1984
The Fluffy Pink Toadstool © Diana Wynne Jones 1979
Auntie Bea's Day Out © Diana Wynne Jones 1979
Carruthers © Diana Wynne Jones 1978
No One © Diana Wynne Jones 1984
Dragon Reserve, Home Eight © Diana Wynne Jones 1984
The Sage of Theare © Diana Wynne Jones 1982

Warlock at the Wheel

The Willing Warlock was a born loser. He lost his magic when Chrestomanci took it away,* and that meant he lost his usual way of making a living. So he decided to take up a life of crime instead by stealing a motor car, because he loved motor cars, and selling it. He found a beautiful car in Wolvercote High Street, but he lost his head when a policeman saw him trying to pick the lock and cycled up to know what he was doing. He ran.

The policeman pedalled after him, blowing his whistle, and the Willing Warlock climbed over the nearest wall and ran again, with the whistle still sounding, until he arrived in the backyard of a one-time Accredited Witch who was a friend of his. 'What shall I do?' he panted.

'How should I know?' said the Accredited Witch. 'I'm not used to doing without magic any more than you are. The only soul I know who's still in business is a French wizard in Shepherd's Bush.'

'Tell me his address,' said the Willing Warlock.

The Accredited Witch told him. 'But it won't do you a scrap of good,' she said unhelpfully. 'Jean-Pierre always charges the earth. Now I'll thank you to get

*See *Charmed Life* by Diana Wynne Jones.

5

out of here before you bring the police down on me too.'

The Willing Warlock went out of the Witch's front door into Coven Street and blenched at the sound of police whistles still shrilling in the distance. Since it seemed to him that he had no time to waste, he hurried to the nearest toyshop and parted with his last half-crown for a toy pistol. Armed with this, he walked into the first Post Office he came to. 'Your money or your life,' he said to the Postmistress. The Willing Warlock was a bulky young man who always looked as if he needed to shave and the Postmistress was sure he was a desperate character. She let him clear out her safe. The Willing Warlock put the money and the pistol in his pocket and hailed a taxi in which he drove all the way to Shepherd's Bush, feeling this was the next best thing to having a car of his own. It cost a lot, but he arrived at the French wizard's office still with £273 6s 4d in his pocket.

The French wizard shrugged in a very French way. 'What is it you expect me to do for you, my friend? Me, I try not to offend the police. If you wish me to help it will cost you.'

'A hundred pounds,' said the Willing Warlock. 'Hide me somehow.'

Jean-Pierre did another shrug. 'For that money,' he said, 'I could hide you two ways. I could turn you into a small round stone –'

'No thanks,' said the Willing Warlock.

' – and keep you in a drawer,' said Jean-Pierre. 'Or I could send you to another world entirely. I could even send you to a world where you would have your magic again –'

'Have my magic?' exclaimed the Willing Warlock.

' – but that would cost you twice as much,' said

Jean-Pierre. 'Yes, naturally you could have your magic again, if you went somewhere where Chrestomanci has no power. The man is not all-powerful.'

'Then I'll go to one of those places,' said the Willing Warlock.

'Very well.' In a bored sort of way, Jean-Pierre picked up a pack of cards and fanned them out. 'Choose a card. This decides which world you will grace with your blue chin.' As the Willing Warlock stretched out his hand to take a card, Jean-Pierre moved them out of reach. 'Whatever world it is,' he said, 'the money there will be quite different from your pounds, shillings and pence. You might as well give me all you have.'

So the Willing Warlock handed over all his £273 6s 4d. Then he was allowed to pick a card. It was the ten of clubs. Not a bad card, the Willing Warlock thought. He was no Fortune Teller, of course, but he knew the ten of clubs meant that someone would bully somebody. He decided that he would be the one doing the bullying, and handed back the card. Jean-Pierre tossed all the cards carelessly down on a table. The Willing Warlock just had time to see that every single one was the ten of clubs, before he found himself still in Shepherd's Bush, but in another world entirely.

He was standing in what seemed to be a car park beside a big road. On that road, more cars than he had ever seen in his life were rushing past, together with lorries and the occasional big red bus. There were cars standing all round him. This was a good world indeed! The Willing Warlock sniffed the delicious smell of petrol and turned to the nearest parked car to see how it worked. It looked rather different from the one he had tried to steal in

7

Wolvercote. Experimentally, he made a magic pass over its bonnet. To his delight, the bonnet promptly sprang open an inch or so. The French wizard had not lied. He had his magic back.

The Willing Warlock was just about to heave up the bonnet and plunge into the mysteries beneath, when he saw a large lady in uniform, with a yellow band round her cap, tramping meaningly towards him. She must be a policewoman. Now he had his magic back, the Willing Warlock did not panic. He simply let go of the bonnet and sauntered casually away. Rather to his surprise, the policewoman did not follow him. She just gave him a look of deep contempt and tucked a message of some kind behind the wiper of the car.

All the same, the Willing Warlock felt it prudent to go on walking. He walked to another street, looking at cars all the time, until something made him look up. In front of him was a grand marble building. CITY BANK, it said, in rich gold letters. Now here, thought the Willing Warlock, was a better way to get a car than simply stealing it. If he robbed this bank, he could buy a car of his very own. He took the toy pistol out of his pocket and went in through the grand door.

Inside it was very hushed and polite and calm. Though there were quite a lot of people there, waiting in front of the cashiers or walking about in the background, nobody seemed to notice the Willing Warlock standing uncertainly waving his pistol. He was forced to go and push the nearest queue of people aside and point the pistol at the lady behind the glass there. 'Money or your life,' he said.

They seemed to notice him then. Somebody screamed. The lady behind the glass went white and put her thumb on a button near her cash-drawer. 'How – how much money sir?' she faltered.

'All of it,' said the Willing Warlock. 'Quickly.' Maybe, he thought afterwards, that was a bit greedy. But it seemed so easy. Everyone, on both sides of the glassed-in counter, was standing frozen, staring at him, afraid of the pistol. And the lady readily opened her cash-drawer and began counting out wads of five-pound-notes, fumbling with haste and eagerness.

While she was doing it, the door of the bank opened and someone came in. The Willing Warlock glanced over his shoulder and saw it was only a small man in a pin-striped suit, who seemed to be staring like everybody else. The lady was actually passing the Willing Warlock the first bundle of money, when the small man shouted out in a very big voice, 'Don't be a fool! He's only joking. That's a toy pistol!'

At once everyone near turned on the Willing Warlock. Three men tried to grab him. An old lady swung her handbag and clouted him round the head. 'Take that, you thief!' A bell began to ring loudly. And, worse still, an unholy howling started somewhere outside, coming closer and closer. 'That's the police coming!' screamed the old lady, and she went for the Willing Warlock again.

The Willing Warlock turned and ran, with everyone trying to stop him and getting in his way. The last person who got in his way was the small man in the pin-striped suit. He took hold of the Willing Warlock's sleeve and said, 'Wait a minute – '

The Willing Warlock was so desperate by then that he fired the toy pistol at him. A stream of water came out of it and caught the small man in one eye, drenching his smart suit. The small man ducked and let go. The Willing Warlock burst out through the door of the bank. The howling outside was hideous. It was coming from a white car labelled POLICE, with a blue flashing light on top, which was racing down the street towards him. There was rather a nice car parked by the kerb, facing towards the police car. A big, shiny, expensive car. Even in his panic, and wondering how the police had been fetched so quickly, that car caught the Willing Warlock's eye. As the police car screamed to a stop and policemen started to jump out of it, the Willing Warlock tore open the door of the nice car, jumped into the seat behind the steering-wheel, and set it going in a burst of desperate magic.

Behind him, the policemen jumped back into their car, which then did a screaming U-turn and came after him. The Willing Warlock saw them coming in a little mirror somebody had thoughtfully fixed to the windscreen. He flung the nice car round a corner out of sight. But the police car followed. The Willing Warlock screamed round another corner, and another. But the police car stuck to him like a leech. The Willing Warlock realized that he had better spare a little magic from making the car go in order to make the car look different. So, as he screamed round yet another corner into the main road he had first seen, he put out his last ounce of magic and turned the car bright pink. To his relief, the police car went past him and roared away into the distance.

The Willing Warlock relaxed a little. He had a nice car of his own now and he seemed to be safe for the moment. But he still had to learn how to make the thing go properly, instead of by magic, and, as he soon discovered, there seemed to be all sorts of other rules to driving that he had never even imagined. For one thing, all the cars kept to the left-hand side, and

10

motorists seemed to get very annoyed when they found a large pink car coming towards them on the other side of the road. Then there were some streets where all the cars seemed to be coming towards the pink car, and the people in those cars shook their fists and pointed and hooted at the Willing Warlock. Then again, sometimes there were lights at crossroads, and people did not seem to like you going past them when they were red.

The Willing Warlock was not very clever, but he did realize quite soon that cars were not often pink. A pink car that broke all these rules was bound to be noticed. So, while he drove on and on, looking for some quiet street where he could learn how the car really worked, he sought about for some other way to disguise the car. He saw that all cars had a plate in front and behind, with letters and numbers on. That made it easy. He changed the front number plate to WW100 and the back one to XYZ123 and let the car return to its nice shiny grey colour and drove soberly on till he found some back streets lined with quiet houses. By this time, he was quite tired. He had never had much magic and he was out of practice anyway. He was glad to stop and look for the knob that made the engine go.

There were rows of knobs, but none of them seemed to be the one he wanted. One knob squirted water all over the front window. Another opened the side windows and brought wet windy air sighing in. Another flashed lights. Yet another made a loud hooting, which made the Willing Warlock jump. People would notice! He became panicky, and found his neck going hot and cold in gusts, with a specially cold, panicky spot in the middle, at the back, just above his collar.

He tried another knob. That played music. The next knob made voices speak. 'Over and out . . . Yes. Pink. I don't know how he got a respray that quick, but it's definitely him . . .' The Willing Warlock, in even more of a panic, realized he was listening to the police by magic, and that they were still hunting him. In his panic, he pressed another knob, which made wipers start furiously waving across the windscreen, wiping off the water the first knob had squirted.

'Doh!' said the Willing Warlock, and put up his hand irritably to rub that panicky cold spot at the back of his neck.

The cold place was connected to a long warm hairy muzzle. Whatever owned the muzzle objected to being wiped away. It let out a deep bass growl and a blast of warm smelly air.

The Willing Warlock snatched his hand away. In his terror, he pressed another button, which caused the seat he was in to collapse gently backwards until he was lying on his back. He found himself staring up into the face of the largest dog he had ever seen. It was a great pepper-coloured brute, with white fangs to match the size of the rest of it. Evidently he had stolen a dog as well as a car.

'Grrrrr,' repeated the dog. It bent its great head until the noise vibrated the Willing Warlock's skull like a road drill, and sniffed his face loudly.

'Get off,' said the Willing Warlock tremulously.

Worse followed. Something surged in the back seat beside the huge dog. A small, shrill voice, sounding very sleepy, said, 'Why have we stopped for, Daddy?'

'Oh my *gawd*!' said the Willing Warlock. He turned his eyes gently sideways under the great dog's face. Sure enough, there was a child on the back seat

12

beside the dog, a rather small child with reddish hair and a slobbery sleepy face.

'You're not my Daddy,' this child said accusingly.

The Willing Warlock rather liked children on the whole, but he knew he would have to get rid of this one somehow. To steal a car and a dog and a child would probably put him in prison for life. People really did not like you stealing children. Frantically he reached forward and pushed knobs. Lights lit, wipers swatted and unswatted, voices spoke, a hooter sounded, but at last he pushed the right one and the seat rose gracefully upright again. He used his magic on the rear door and it sprang open. 'Out,' he said. 'Both of you. Get out and wait and your Daddy will find you.'

Dog and child turned and stared at the open door. Their faces turned back to the Willing Warlock, puzzled and slightly indignant. It was their car, after all.

The Willing Warlock tried a bit of coaxing. 'Get out. Nice dog. Good boy.'

'Grrrr,' said the dog, and the child said, 'I'm not a boy.'

'I meant the dog,' the Willing Warlock said hastily. The dog's growl enlarged to a rumble that shook the car. Perhaps the dog was not a boy either. The Willing Warlock knew when he was beaten. It was a pity, when it was such a nice car, but this world was full of cars. Provided he made sure the next one was empty, he could steal one any time he liked. He slammed the rear door shut and started to open his own.

The dog was too quick for him. Before he had reached for the handle, its great teeth were fastened into the shoulder of his jacket, right through the cloth. He could feel them digging into his skin underneath.

13

And it growled harder than ever. 'Let go,' the Willing Warlock said, without hope, and sat very still.

'Go on driving,' commanded the child.

'Why?' said the Willing Warlock.

'Because I like driving in cars,' said the child. 'Towser will let you go when you drive.'

'I don't know how to make the car go,' the Willing Warlock said sullenly.

'Stupid,' said the child. 'Daddy uses those keys there, and he pushes on the pedals with his feet.'

Towser backed this up with another growl, and dug his teeth in a little. Towser clearly knew his job, and his job seemed to be to back up anything the child said. The Willing Warlock sighed, thinking of years in prison, but he found the keys and located the pedals. He turned the keys. He pushed on the pedals. The engine started with a roar. Then another voice spoke. 'You have forgotten to fasten your seatbelt,' it said. 'I cannot proceed until you do so.'

It was here that the Willing Warlock realized that his troubles had only just begun. The car was bullying him now. He had no idea where the seatbelt was, but it is amazing what you can do if a mouthful of white fangs are fastened into your shoulder. The Willing Warlock found the seatbelt. He did it up. He found a lever that said *forwards* and pushed it. He pressed on pedals. The engine roared, but nothing else happened. 'You are wasting petrol,' the car told him acidly. 'Release the hand-brake. I cannot pro -' The Willing Warlock found a sort of stick in the floor and moved it. It snapped like a crocodile and the car jerked. 'You are wasting petrol,' the car said, boringly. 'Release the footbrake. I cannot proceed –'

Luckily, since Towser was growling even louder than the car, the Willing Warlock took his left foot off a pedal first. They shot off down the road. 'You are wasting petrol,' the car told him.

'Oh shut up,' the Willing Warlock said. But nothing shut the car up, he discovered, except not pressing so hard on the right-hand pedal. Towser, on the other hand, seemed satisfied as soon as the car moved. He let go of the Willing Warlock and loomed behind him on the back seat, while the child sat and chanted 'Go on, go on, go on driving.'

The Willing Warlock kept on driving. There is nothing else you can do if a child, a dog the size of Towser, and a car, all combine to make you. At least the car was easy to drive. All the Willing Warlock had to do was sit there not pressing the pedal too much and keep turning into the emptiest streets. He had time to think. He knew the dog's name. If he could find out the child's name, then he could work a spell on them both to make them let him go.

'What's your name?' he asked, turning into a wide straight road with room for three cars abreast in it.

'Jemima Jane,' said the child. 'Go on, go on, go on driving.'

The Willing Warlock drove, muttering a spell. While he did, Towser made a flowing sort of jump and landed in the passenger seat beside him, where he sat in a royal way, staring out at the road. The Willing Warlock cowered away from him and finished the spell in a gabble. The beast was as big as a lion!

'You are wasting petrol,' remarked the car.

Perhaps these things caused the Willing Warlock to muddle the spell. All that happened was that Towser turned invisible.

There was an instant shriek from the back seat. 'Where's Towser?'

The invisible space on the front passenger seat

15

growled horribly. The Willing Warlock did not know where its teeth were. He hurriedly revoked the spell. Towser loomed beside him, looking reproachful.

'You're not do that again!' said Jemima Jane.

'I won't if we all get out and walk,' the Willing Warlock said cunningly.

A silence met this suggestion, with an undercurrent of snarl to it. The Willing Warlock gave up for the moment and kept on driving. There were no houses by the road any more, only trees, grass and a few cows, and the road stretched into the distance, endlessly. The nice grey car, labelled WW100 in front and XYZ123 behind, zoomed gently onwards for nearly an hour. The sun began setting in gory clouds, behind some low green hills.

'I want my supper,' announced Jemima Jane. At the word *supper*, Towser yawned and started to dribble. He turned to look thoughtfully at the Willing Warlock, obviously wondering which bits of him tasted best. 'Towser's hungry too,' said Jemima Jane.

The Willing Warlock turned his eyes sideways to look at Towser's great pink tongue draped over Towser's large white fangs. 'I'll stop at the first place we see,' he said obligingly. He began turning over schemes for giving both of them – not to speak of the car – the slip the moment they allowed him to stop. If he made himself invisible, so that the dog could not find him –

He seemed to be in luck. Just then a large blue notice that said HARBURY SERVICES came into view, with a picture of a knife and fork underneath. The Willing Warlock turned into it with a squeal of tyres. 'You are wasting petrol,' the car protested. The Willing Warlock took no notice. He stopped with a jolt among a lot of other cars, turned himself invisible

16

and tried to jump out. But he had forgotten the seatbelt. It held him in place long enough for Towser to fix his fangs in the sleeve of his coat, and that seemed to be enough to make Towser turn invisible too. 'You have forgotten to set the handbrake,' said the car.

'Doh!' snarled the Willing Warlock miserably, and put the handbrake on. It was not easy, with Towser's invisible fangs grating his arm.

'You're to fetch me lots and lots,' Jemima Jane said. It did not seem to trouble her that both of them had vanished. 'Towser, make sure he brings me an ice-cream.'

The Willing Warlock climbed out of the car, lugging the invisible Towser. He tried some more cunning. 'Come with me and show me which ice-cream you want,' he called back. Several people in the car park looked round to see where the invisible voice was coming from.

'I want to stay in the car. I'm tired,' whined Jemima Jane.

The invisible teeth fastened in the Willing Warlock's sleeve rumbled a little. Invisible dribble ran on his hand. 'Oh all right,' he said, and set off for the restaurant, accompanied by four invisible heavy paws.

Maybe it was a good thing they were both invisible. There was a big sign on the door: NO DOGS. And the Willing Warlock still had no money. He went to the long counter and picked up pies and scones with the hand Towser left him free. He stuffed them into his pocket so that they would become invisible too. Someone pointed to the Danish pastry he picked up next and screamed, 'Look! A ghost!' Then there were screams further down the counter. The Willing

17

Warlock looked. A very large chocolate gateau, with a snout-shaped piece missing from it, was trotting at chest-level across the dining area. Towser was helping himself too. People backed away, yelling. The gateau broke into a gallop and barged out through the glass doors with a splat. At the same moment, someone grabbed the Danish pasty from the Willing Warlock's hand.

It was the girl behind the cash-desk, who was not afraid of ghosts. 'You're the Invisible Man or something,' she said. 'Give that back.'

The Willing Warlock panicked again and ran after the gateau. He meant to go on running, as fast as he could, in the opposite direction to the nice car. But as soon as he barged through the door, he found the gateau waiting for him, lying on the ground. A warning growl and hot breath on his hand suggested that he pick the gateau up and come along. Teeth in his trouser-leg backed up this suggestion. Dismally, the Willing Warlock obeyed.

'Where's my ice-cream?' Jemima Jane asked ungratefully.

'There wasn't any,' said the Willing Warlock as Towser herded him into the car. He threw the gateau, the scones and a pork pie on to the back seat. 'Be thankful for what you've got.'

'Why?' asked Jemima Jane.

The Willing Warlock gave up. He turned himself visible again and sat in the driving seat to eat the other pork pie. He could feel Towser snuffing him from time to time make sure he stayed there. In between, he could hear Towser eating. Towser made such a noise that the Willing Warlock was glad he was invisible. He looked to make sure. And there was Towser, visible again in all his hugeness, sitting in the back seat licking his vast chops. As for Jemima Jane – the Willing Warlock had to look away quickly. She was chocolate all over. There was a river of chocolate down her front and more plastered into her red curls like mud.

'Why aren't you going on driving for?' Jemima Jane demanded. Towser at once surged to his huge feet to back up the demand.

'I am, I am!' the Willing Warlock said, hastily starting the engine.

'You have forgotten to fasten your seatbelt,' the car reminded him priggishly. And as the car moved forward, it added, 'It is now lighting-up time. You require headlights.'

The Willing Warlock started the wipers, rolled down windows, played music, and finally managed to turn on the lights. He drove back on to the big road, hating all three of them. And drove. Jemima Jane stood up on the back seat behind him. The gateau had made her distressingly lively. She wanted to talk. She grabbed one of the Willing Warlock's ears in a sticky chocolate hand for balance, and breathed gateau-fumes and questions into his other ear.

'Why did you take our car for? What are all those prickles on your chin for? Why don't you like me holding your nose for? Why don't you smell nice? Where are we going to? Shall we drive in the car all night?' and many more such questions.

The Willing Warlock was forced to answer all these questions in the right way. If he did not answer, Jemima Jane dragged at his hair, or twisted his ear, or took hold of his nose. If the answer he gave did not please Jemima Jane, Towser rose up growling, and the Willing Warlock had quickly to think of a better answer. It was not long before he was as plastered with chocolate as Jemima Jane was. He thought that it was not possible for a person to be more unhappy.

He was wrong. Towser suddenly stood up and staggered about the back seat, making odd noises.

'Towser's going to go sick,' Jemima Jane said.

The Willing Warlock squealed to a halt on the hard shoulder and threw all four doors open wide. Towser would have to get out, he thought. Then he could drive straight off again and leave Towser by the roadside.

As he thought that, Towser landed heavily on top of him. Sitting on the Willing Warlock, he got rid of the gateau on to the edge of the motorway. It took him some time. Meanwhile, the Willing Warlock wondered if Towser was actually as heavy as a cow, or whether he only felt that way.

'Now go on, go on driving,' Jemima Jane said, when Towser at last had finished.

The Willing Warlock obeyed. He drove on. Then it was the car's turn. It flashed a red light at him. 'You are running out of petrol,' it remarked.

'Good,' said the Willing Warlock feelingly.

'Go on driving,' said Jemima Jane, and Towser, as usual, backed her up.

The Willing Warlock drove on through the night. A new and unpleasant smell now filled the car. It did not mix well with chocolate. The Willing Warlock supposed it must be Towser. He drove, and the car boringly repeated its remark about petrol, until, as they passed a sign saying BENTWELL SERVICES, the car suddenly changed its tune and said, 'You have started on the reserve tank.' Then it became quite talkative and added, 'You have petrol for ten more miles only. You are running out of petrol . . .'

'I heard you,' said the Willing Warlock. 'I shall have

20

to stop,' he told Jemima Jane and Towser, with great relief. Then, to stop Jemima Jane telling him to drive on, and because the new smell was mixing with the chocolate worse than ever, he said, 'And what is this smell in here?'

'Me,' Jemima Jane said, rather defiantly. 'I went in my pants. It's your fault. You didn't take me to the Ladies.'

At which Towser at once sprang up, growling, and the car added, 'You are running out of petrol.'

The Willing Warlock groaned aloud and went squealing into BENTWELL SERVICES. The car told him reproachfully that he was wasting petrol and then added that he was running out of it, but the Willing Warlock was too far gone to attend to it. He sprang out of the car and once more tried to run away. Towser sprang out after him and fastened his teeth in the Willing Warlock's now tattered trouser-leg. And Jemima Jane scrambled out after Towser.

'Take me to the Ladies,' she said. 'You have to change my knickers. My clean ones are in the bag in the back.'

'I can't take you to the Ladies!' the Willing Warlock said. He had no idea what to do. What *did* one do? You have one grown-up male Warlock, one female child and one dog fastened to the Warlock's trouser-leg that might be male or female. Did you go to the Gents or the Ladies? The Willing Warlock just did not know. He had to settle for doing it publicly in the car park. It made him ill. It was the last straw. Jemima Jane gave him loud directions in a ringing bossy voice. Towser growled steadily. As he struggled with the gruesome task, the Willing Warlock heard people gathering round, sniggering. He hardly cared. He was a broken Warlock by then. When he looked up to find

21

himself in a ring of policemen, and the small man in the pin-striped suit standing just beside him, he felt nothing but extreme relief. 'I'll come quietly,' he said.

'Hello, Daddy!' Jemima Jane shouted. She suddenly looked enchanting, in spite of the chocolate. And Towser changed character too and fawned and gambolled round the small man, squeaking like a puppy.

The small man picked up Jemima Jane, chocolate and all, and looked forbiddingly at the Willing Warlock. 'If you've harmed Prudence, or the dog either,' he said, 'you're for it, you know.'

'Harmed!' the Willing Warlock said hysterically. 'That child's the biggest bully in the world – bar that car or that dog! And the dog's a thief too! *I'm* the one that's harmed! Anyway, she said her name was Jemima Jane.'

'That just a jingle I taught her, to prevent people trying name-magic,' the small man said, laughing rather. 'The dog has a secret name anyway. All Kathayack Demon Dogs do. Do you know who I am am, Warlock?'

'No,' said the Willing Warlock, trying not to look respectfully at the fawning Towser. He had heard of Demon Dogs. The beast probably had more magic than he did.

'Kathusa,' said the man. 'Financial wizard. I'm Chrestomanci's agent in this world. That crook Jean-Pierre keeps sending people here and they all get into trouble. It's my job to pick them up. I was coming into the bank to help you, Warlock, and you go and pinch my car.'

'Oh,' said the Willing Warlock. The policemen coughed and began to close in. He resigned himself to a long time in prison.

But Kathusa held up a hand to stop the policemen.

'See here, Warlock,' he said, 'you have a choice. I need a man to look after my cars and exercise Towser. You can do that and go straight, or you can go to prison. Which is it to be?'

It was a terrible choice. Towser met the Willing Warlock's eye and licked his lips. The Willing Warlock decided he preferred prison. But Jemima Jane – or rather Prudence – turned to the policemen, beaming. 'He's going to look after me and Towser,' she announced. 'He likes his nose being pulled.'

The Willing Warlock tried not to groan.

The Plague of Peacocks

From the moment the Platts came to Chipping Hanbury everyone knew they were Caring People. They bought the old cottage up Weavers Close beside the field where the children went to cycle and play football. Mr Platt took the cottage apart all by himself and built it up again and painted it white. Mrs Platt took the garden apart and painted everything there white too.

When they had done that, they began caring for Chipping Hanbury.

Mr Platt brought out a news sheet which he called *Hanbury Village News* and put a copy through everyone's door. The copies were addressed to everyone by their first names in the most friendly way: the Willises' was to Glenda and Jack, the Moores' to Lily and Tony, the Dougals' to Marcia and Ken, and so on. Everyone wondered how Mr Platt knew their names, and whether he was right to call Hanbury a village when it was really just a place on the edge of London. The news sheet was full of kind advice about how Hanbury needed more street lights and a bus shelter and tidier front gardens. Weavers Pond was full of rubbish too, Mr Platt said reproachfully, and the football field ought to be a proper sports centre. People like Glenda and Jack, who had private incomes, really ought to see about cleaning the place up.

'Why does he think we have private incomes?' said Mrs Willis. 'Because the children have ponies?' Mrs Willis did typing for people in order to pay for the ponies and she was rather hurt.

Meanwhile, Mrs Platt was caring for animals. The first to go was the Dougal's cat Sooty. Then the Deans' dog Lambert. Then Holly Smith's angora rabbit. Mrs Platt called on the Dougals, the Deans and the Smiths and explained at length that she had found the animal wandering about, and it might have gone in the road, and there was such a lot of traffic these days, and one should keep pets tied up. Mrs Platt was thin, with intense grey eyes, and she bent forwards nervously when she talked, and twisted her hands together. People found it hard to interrupt her when she was so worried. But after an hour or so, the Dougals and the Deans and the Smiths plucked up courage to ask what had happened to their animals. Mrs Platt explained that she had put them in the car and Mr Platt had driven them to a vet he knew, to have them put down.

Mr Platt's next news sheet had a sorrowful page on how badly people looked after their animals. The other pages were about the new greenhouses Mr Platt was building behind the cottage. Mr Platt was a thick energetic man with a beard and juicy red lips, and he had a passion for building greenhouses. When he was not doing that, he was either standing with his head back and his chest out admiring the latest greenhouse, or he was walking round Hanbury looking for news to put in his news sheet. He was walking in Hart Lane when Sarah Willis got run away with by her pony.

What made Chunter bolt was a mystery. Sarah

always said he had seen Mr Platt and was afraid of being taken to the vet too. Anyway, there was Chunter hammering along the road, striking frantic sparks from it with his hooves, with Sarah clinging on for dear life, when Mr Platt came jumping out of the hedge and swung on Chunter's bridle.

'Thanks,' said Sarah, when Chunter had stopped.

'You should never, never let a pony gallop on a tarmac road,' said Mr Platt. 'I don't think anyone has explained to you: it ruins their feet and jars their legs.'

'But I didn't – !' said Sarah. That was all she managed to say, because Mr Platt proved to be just as good a talker as his wife, and he walked back to the house with her, holding Chunter's bridle and explaining gently how you should treat a pony. 'I think I must come inside and explain to Glenda that you shouldn't ride without proper supervision,' he said when they got there. And he did. When he had done that, he went out to look at the barn where the ponies lived and came back to tell Mrs Willis that it was not suitable for ponies.

Mrs Willis was typing somebody's book about the history of Poland, full of names like Mrzchtochky, and she left out several Zs. 'I shall go mad,' she said.

'Don't worry,' said Sarah. 'There's always Daniel Emanuel.'

No one had yet told the Platts about Daniel Emanuel. This was odd, because Daniel Emanuel was well known to be interested in animals too. Only the week before, he had fallen out of the oak tree in the football field trying to catch a squirrel. Last year he had cut himself on rusty iron wading into Weavers Pond after a duck and nearly died of tetanus, because he had heard you could eat ducks.

Mrs Platt met Daniel Emanuel first. She was

26

coming home after caring for the Moores' budgie. She had found it on her windowsill. By this time, she had noticed that people did not quite like it when she took their pets to the vet. So she took the budgie home. 'Look, Lily,' she explained, 'I've cut his wings for you, ever so neatly, so that he won't be able to fly away again.'

'How kind!' Mrs Moore said bitterly, thinking she would have to keep the cat in the yard in case Mrs Platt cared for the cat too. 'You'll have to keep the budgie in your bedroom,' she said to her son Terry. 'I hope Daniel Emanuel does something to the Platts soon!'

Mrs Platt had got halfway home, to the bottom of the main road, when she saw, to her horror, a four-year-old boy walk out into the traffic. A bus bucked to a stop almost on top of him. Two cars missed him by two separate miracles. Mrs Platt rushed into the road and seized the child's arm. 'Who are you, little man? Does your Mummy know you're out?'

He looked up at her. 'I'm Daniel Emanuel of course,' he said. He had curly hair and long eyelashes and a band of freckles across his nose.

'Where do you live?' said Mrs Platt.

Daniel Emanuel did not seem to be sure. He let Mrs Platt lead him round Chipping Hanbury. She seemed to want to, and he felt like a walk anyway. After an hour or so though, she began to bother him. She kept asking things and calling him 'little man'. The only little men Daniel Emanuel had ever heard of were the dwarves in Snow White, and he began to be afraid he would not grow any more. He took Mrs Platt home so that he could ask Linda.

Mrs Platt looked at the O'Flahertys' tall ramshackle

house with pieces of car lying about the front garden under the washing-line. Children were running and screaming, and Mrs O'Flaherty was anxiously looking over the front gate. 'This is a Problem Family,' Mrs Platt said to herself, 'and I must care for them.'

'Daniel Emanuel!' everyone in the garden screamed.

'He was walking in the traffic,' Mrs Platt explained. She had meant to have a long talk with Mrs O'Flaherty about her problems, but Mrs O'Flaherty was so glad to see Daniel Emanuel safe that she took him straight indoors. 'No manners either,' Mrs Platt said sorrowfully.

Indoors, Mrs O'Flaherty said, 'You naughty boy!' and raised her fist. Daniel Emanuel's face screwed up miserably. 'Oh, I can't hit him!' said Mrs O'Flaherty and she took her fist down. Daniel Emanuel unscrewed his face and beamed. 'Linda,' said Mrs O'Flaherty, 'why did you let him go in the road?'

Linda was five, and the only one who knew how to manage Daniel Emanuel. She shrugged. There were times when even she could not stop Daniel Emanuel. 'He can think,' she explained, 'and the cars just stop.'

'He may think they will, but they don't,' said Mrs O'Flaherty and hurried away to get lunch. A mother who had seven children and a husband who spends his spare time stock-car racing has not quite time to understand everything.

'Am I a little man?' Daniel Emanuel asked Linda anxiously.

Linda knew what he meant. 'Not you!' she said. 'You'll grow bigger than Dad.'

28

Daniel Emanuel was much relieved. He was not sure he liked Mrs Platt. She said things that were not true.

Mr Platt's next news sheet had a lot in it about Problem Families.

'Oh good,' said Mrs Willis to Sarah and James. 'They've met Daniel Emanuel.'

Next time Daniel Emanuel gave Linda the slip he went to look at the Platts' cottage. He thought it was lovely. The stones round the flowers were painted white. There was a white wheelbarrow on the front lawn with flowers planted in it which bothered Daniel Emanuel. Flowers should grow in the ground. Daniel Emanuel took the flowers out carefully and tipped the earth on the grass. He found Mr Platt's golf clubs in the porch and dug a hole for the flowers with them in front of the porch. He put the flowers in the hole and carefully opened the tap in the rainwater butt to give the flowers a drink. Then he found a pot of white paint in the porch and thought he ought to give the hole a white rim like the other flowerbeds. When Mr Platt came round the house from building his fourth greenhouse, he found Daniel Emanuel squatting in a river using a bent golf club as a paintbrush.

Mr Platt took Daniel Emanuel in a stern kind hand and led him home, talking gently to him about how wicked he was. Daniel Emanuel seemed a little vague about what wicked meant. Mr Platt explained by telling him stories, and one of the stories was Daniel in the Lions' Den.

'Oh Daniel Emanuel!' said Mrs O'Flaherty when she opened the door. Daniel Emanuel was earth-coloured with streaks of white. Mr Platt was shocked to see that Mrs O'Flaherty had been reading a book while she cooked lunch. She had two favourite books which she read turn and turn about to keep her sane: this one was *The Mill on the Floss*; the other was *The Count of Monte Cristo*. She knew both so well that she could do most things while she was reading.

Mr Platt explained what Daniel Emanuel had done and gave Mrs O'Flaherty long and patient advice on how to bring up children, until Mrs O'Flaherty smelt the potatoes burning and snatched Daniel Emanuel up and ran. 'What a feckless woman,' Mr Platt said sadly.

Mrs O'Flaherty was so annoyed about the potatoes that Daniel Emanuel barely got scolded. 'Where's any lions?' he asked Linda as soon as he was free.

'Aren't any,' said Linda. 'Only in cages in the Zoo.'

The next day, Daniel Emanuel set out to find himself a cage of lions.

There are no lions in Chipping Hanbury. The only large beasts are Sarah Willis's Chunter and James Willis's Ben. Daniel Emanuel was seen by James standing in the doorway of the ponies' barn. 'Is this a den?' Daniel Emanuel asked.

'No,' said James. 'It's a stall.'

Daniel Emanuel nodded and went away. He was next heard of eight miles away in Abbots Hanbury. How he got there Daniel Emanuel never said, but there he was. He was in a pen in the cattle market with a hundred pigs, angrily shouting, 'Bite me!' His father was home when the police telephoned. He drove his newest car to Abbots Hanbury and fetched Daniel Emanuel away. Since Mr O'Flaherty was the only person in the world that Daniel Emanuel was afraid of, Daniel Emanuel arrived home very sore and sullen. 'I don't like Platts,' he told Linda.

Both the Platts were very concerned about Daniel Emanuel. Mr Platt went to see Mr O'Flaherty to tell him Daniel Emanuel needed special care, and the Dougals saw him leave again rather quickly. Mrs Platt went to speak to Mrs Willis. 'Glenda,' she said, 'I think we two should get together and care for our Problem Family. The O'Flahertys, you know.'

This time, Mrs Willis was typing someone's experimental novel. It went down the page in two columns which said the same thing, but not quite, and it had to catch the five o'clock post. 'I don't think they're a problem,' she said. 'Ask James and Sarah. Their main friends are Patrick and Thelma O'Flaherty. Do let me catch the post.' But Mrs Platt stayed persuading Mrs Willis till four o'clock. At four-thirty Mr Platt arrived with some brochures, saying that he and Mrs Platt thought Mrs Willis ought to be using a word processor. When Sarah and James and Mr Willis came home just after five, Mr Platt was still there and Mrs Willis was in tears.

'Do something!' said Mr Willis.

James and Sarah saddled their ponies and went drumming away down the bridle path to the football field where Thelma and Patrick were riding their bicycles. 'What is it?' said Patrick, propping himself on the hedge.

'Make Daniel Emanuel do something to the Platts,' said Sarah.

'You can borrow the ponies and we'll go on a bike-and-pony trek if you do,' said James.

Thelma and Patrick looked wistfully at one another. It was an offer they couldn't refuse. It cost Patrick a lot to say, 'We can't make him do anything.' And it cost Thelma just as much to add, 'Linda's his manager.'

'Ask her, and we'll do the trek anyway,' said Sarah.

During the last month, Linda had been rather

31

pestered. Holly Smith, Terry Moore and Alastair Dougal has also made offers that couldn't be refused to Brendan, Maureen and Brian O'Flaherty. 'He's not ready to do anything yet,' she told Thelma and Patrick. 'But I'll try.'

Next Saturday, Sarah and James kept their promise and the trek set off to Beacon Hill. Linda kept hers by taking Daniel Emanuel for a walk in Weavers Close. But it was one of Daniel Emanuel's saintly days. Nothing happened, except that Mrs Platt saw them and hurried out saying, 'Little children like you oughtn't to be out alone!' She brought them inside the cottage, where it was neat and plain and brown, and made them sit down. Linda looked hopefully round for biscuits at least, but Mrs Platt sat down too and told them the story of Jesus. Linda knew it. She had been sent home from school on her first day crying about Jesus. She turned paler and paler.

'Did it hurt much?' she whispered.

'What, dear?' asked Mrs Platt.

'Being nailed up in a tree,' Linda whispered.

Mrs Platt was rather taken aback. 'Well –' Since she did not know what to tell Linda, she took them back home feeling she had given them both something to think about.

She had. While Mrs O'Flaherty was trying to stop Linda crying, Daniel Emanuel collected four nails, a hammer and some string, and marched off to the oak tree in the football field to find out for himself if it hurt to be crucified.

Luckily for him, he got tangled in the string before he had banged in the first nail properly. Even more luckily, Sarah, James, Patrick and Thelma happened to be coming home only an hour later after an almost perfect day. They heard the thin little wailing, which was all the noise Daniel Emanuel was able to make by then. 'That's Daniel Emanuel!' said Thelma, and managed to make Chunter gallop. And it was lucky the ponies were there. Daniel Emanuel was quite high up, hanging mostly by one arm. They managed to reach him by putting the ponies under the branch, with James, standing on the ponies, one foot on Chunter and one on Ben, boosting Patrick to the branch to cut the string. Sarah held the ponies and Thelma caught Daniel Emanuel as he came down. He hurt a lot, and he was frozen, and he was very angry. 'It's not *good* for people!' he kept saying as he rode home in front of Thelma. They put him to bed, and he brooded. He was very angry with both the Platts. They pretended to be kind and told you bad things.

Mr and Mrs Platt went from house to house with a petition to have the oak tree cut down. They said it was very dangerous.

'Wouldn't it be easier to take Daniel Emanuel to the vet?' Mrs Willis asked sweetly.

Mr Platt didn't follow her meaning at all; but he followed Mr O'Flaherty's meaning when Mr O'Flaherty told him what to do with his petition.

Daniel Emanuel was still brooding. 'He's nearly ready,' Linda told the others. Nearly every day, Daniel Emanuel went round to Weavers Close and stood looking at the cottage thinking what to do. When Mr and Mrs Platt came out to take him home, he had vanished before they got to the road. But one day the Platts went out in their car. Daniel Emanuel wandered through the garden and round the back. He wandered thoughtfully through all the greenhouses. Mr Platt had never stopped building greenhouses. There were six by now. Daniel Emanuel ate tomatoes in one and picked a bunch of flowers in two. He made pies in flowerpots in the other three, thinking, thinking. But none of it gave him any ideas and he went away.

Mr Platt did not want to meet Mr O'Flaherty face to face again. He telephoned and pointed out that Daniel Emanuel was being allowed to run wild. It was not so much the tomatoes, he said, but the child's own good . . . The person the other end rang off. 'Will you come here, Danny!' Mr O'Flaherty roared. Mr Platt would have been shocked at the storm which broke out then.

When it was over, Mr O'Flaherty went out in the car to cool down. Mrs O'Flaherty lay down and read *The Count of Monte Cristo* to calm her nerves. Daniel Emanuel, very sore and sullen, went to watch television.

It was a programme about birds. The hen-bird came tiptoeing on to the screen, thin and brown and nervy, jerking its little head in just the same way that Mrs Platt did when she explained something for your own good. The cock-bird strutted on and bent its neck back just like Mr Platt. Then it spread out a great circle of tail and looked exactly like Mr Platt admiring a greenhouse.

'Platt, Platt!' shrieked Daniel Emanuel and ran to find Linda.

Linda was cooking. She had tipped in a bag of flour and a bag of sugar, and she was trying to crunch in a dozen eggs with a fork before Mrs O'Flaherty stopped reading and found her. 'I'm busy,' she said. But her sleeve was being pulled in a particular way. She went with Daniel Emanuel and a trail of flour and mashed eggshell and looked at the television. 'Peacocks,' she said.

'Platts,' Daniel Emanuel said. He went into the

34

front garden among the pieces of car and thought of a peacock. When the peacock came, it was blue and green and trailed its tail like a filmstar's skirt. It stood in front of a shiny hubcap of a piece of car and looked at itself and admired itself greatly. Daniel Emanuel nodded and thought of a peahen. She tiptoed up like Mrs Platt going after somebody's stray pet. Daniel Emanuel nodded again. 'Peacocks,' he murmured. 'Hundreds and hundreds.' And he thought of himself holding open a gap in the hedge behind Mr Platt's greenhouses to let a long, long line of peacocks and peahens tiptoe through. Hundreds, hundreds . . .

When Mrs O'Flaherty had finished dealing with Linda, she was very relieved to find Daniel Emanuel curled up asleep beside the hubcap of a piece of car. 'Oh, isn't he an angel!' she said.

And the Platts were suddenly overwhelmed with peacocks. They sat in rows on the cottage roof, and the garden was a mass of tiptoeing green and brown, mixed with spreading tails and horrible sudden peacock screams. Peacocks got in the greenhouses. They invaded the house . . . But long before this, Holly Smith had rushed home shouting the news. Mrs Smith telephoned everyone in Chipping Hanbury and all the adults promptly pretended to be ill and sent their children to the football field. Mrs Willis gave up typing for other people and typed instead the news brought by a stream of children on bicycles. James and Sarah cantered from house to house delivering little cryptic notes saying things like: TWO MORE FELL THROUGH THE GREENHOUSES and SHE GOT PECKED and DROPPINGS ALL OVER SOFA and ONE LAID AN EGG IN THEIR LOO and ROOSTING ON TELEPHONE WHEN THEY TRIED TO RING VET.

35

A row of interested heads watched over the hedge when the Platts tried to get their car out and drive a load of peacocks to the vet. The running, the chasing, the shooing, the squawks and clouds of feathers was quite indescribable. Mrs Willis's note summed it up: THEY COULDN'T. So Mr Platt tried going round all the houses asking for help. The peacocks seemed fond of him. Twenty or so followed him faithfully from door to door and drowned his voice with screams when the doors were opened. Mr Platt was sorry to find that everyone opened the door wearing nightclothes and holding a handkerchief to their faces. There seemed to be quite a flu epidemic. So he went home, followed by his procession of birds, and the Platts waited for the peacocks to go away. But they didn't. If anything, they seemed to get more every day.

The Platts stood it for almost a month and then they went away themselves. Everyone recovered from flu in time to wave goodbye to their car as it drove off with peacocks clinging to the roof rack and more hastily waddling and flapping behind. Linda had a marvellous time that day. Mrs O'Flaherty was touched and puzzled at the way everyone seemed to be thinking of treats for Linda and Daniel Emanuel.

The Platts' cottage is still standing empty except for peacocks, but some of the peacocks seem to have lost interest and wandered away. Since then there have been outbreaks of peacocks here and there all round the edges of London. This is because Daniel Emanuel has forgotten about them. He has started school now and has other things to think of.

36

The Fluffy Pink Toadstool

Mother was always having crazes. Since she was a strong-minded lady, this meant that the rest of the family had the crazes too – until, that is, Father put his foot down.

This particular craze started as a Hand-Made craze. About the beginning of the summer holidays, Mother suddenly decided that they were going to do without things which were made in factories. 'We are going to use,' she declared, 'things which are made by people who loved every stitch and nail as they made them.'

This meant that there was suddenly almost no furniture in the house, except the Persian rug in the living-room and the stool Paul had made in Woodwork. The stool wobbled. Paul explained that this was because he had *not* loved every nail as he made it. He still had the bruises. Father told him to shut up, or they would have nothing to sit on at all.

After that, Mother threw away most of their clothes. The clothes she got instead were handwoven and large, and in peculiar colours. Paul was glad it was the holidays, because he would not have dared go to school in them. Nina wept bitterly. Mother had thrown away her pink fluffy slippers, because they were made in a factory. Nina loved those slippers. They had pink fluffy bobbles on the front, which Nina stroked every night before she went to sleep. Father raised an outcry too, and refused to go to the office in his new trousers. They were baggy, green sackcloth sort of things, with pink stripes round the legs. Mother let him keep a pair of office-trousers on condition he wore the baggy ones at weekends. She made all of them wear flat, handmade sandals that fell off when they walked.

The only one who did not mind was Tim. He was too young to care. He wore his floppy, purple tunic quite happily and, when his sandals fell off, he ran about barefoot, until the soles of his feet were as hard as leather, only rather more yellow. He was fascinated by the clothes Mother wore, too. Mother got a long, long skirt, which looked like dirty lace curtains. Tim found he could see Mother's legs walking through the skirt. He followed her about, watching for the moment when she bent down and the net-curtain trailed on the floor. When she stood up again, her feet always went walking up the front of her skirt inside, and she had to stop and walk backwards.

Tim was the only one who did not mind going shopping with Mother that summer. Because, naturally, Mother began insisting on Natural Food. She would trail her grey skirt into the bread-shop, with her handmade basket on her arm, and ask sharply: 'Is your bread stone-ground?'

'Oh no,' said the lady. 'It's made of flour. Wheat ground, you know'.

Mother had almost no sense of humour. She made her own bread after that, and it *was* rather like stones that had been ground.

In the butcher's she asked: 'Has this meat lived a natural life?'

'About as natural as yours, lady,' the butcher said crossly.

Mother swept out of the butcher's and did not buy meat again. She did most of her shopping in the vegetable-shop instead, where she would prod each vegetable and each fruit and ask: 'Has this been grown with natural manure?'

The greengrocer, who found Mother a valuable customer, always assured her that everything was left entirely to Nature. All the same, Mother never bought anything from abroad, because she was not sure that foreigners had the right, Natural ideas.

Soon, there was almost as little food in the house as there was furniture. There were a great many nuts and raisins, because Mother had not noticed that these things come from foreign parts, but almost the only ordinary food was cornflakes. Mother kept on buying cornflakes because it said on the packet: *Made from finest natural ingredients*. But one can get tired of cornflakes quite easily. Father was so tired of them that he used to take all three children for secret trips to the chip-shop. Usually they stopped at the ice-cream van on the corner on the way home, and came back feeling much more satisfied.

It had been a very sunny summer. By the end of it, the brambles at the bottom of the garden were full of ripe blackberries. Mother became inspired. 'We should be living off the Fruits of the Earth,' she said. 'There is nothing more Natural or more nutritious.' She bought a number of books to find out just what Fruits of the Earth were most good for you, and grew very excited. 'We must all go out into the woods and pick things,' she said.

39

'Good,' said Paul, who had by now eaten most of the blackberries in the garden. 'I fancy a blackberry tart.'

'Even with ground-stone pastry,' Nina agreed.

Unfortunately, the nearest woods were ten miles away. Mother would not hear of going by car, because that was not Natural. Her first idea was that they should all cycle there, but she had to give that up when her grey net skirt kept getting tangled in bicycle chain. So she said they must all walk.

'Nonsense,' said Father. 'Tim can't possibly walk twenty miles.'

'Besides,' muttered Paul, 'people grew quite naturally from apes, so everything people do is natural anyway, even cars.'

Before there could be an argument, Father put Tim in the car and told the other two to get in as well. Mother gave in with dignity, and they all drove to the woods.

There, Mother became strong-minded again. She refused to let them pick blackberries, because there were blackberries at home. She gave Paul and Nina a handmade basket each and set them to pick sloes. She set Father to gathering wild onions on a sunny bank. She herself, with Tim trotting beside her, wandered through the shadier parts of the wood with a shiny new book called *Toadstools for Dinner* open in front of her nose. From time to time she would pounce on an ear-like fungus growing on a tree. 'These are wonderfully nutritious!' she would call out. 'You beat them with a hammer, and then they taste almost like turnips.'

Tim got the idea. He pattered happily about, bringing Mother yellow toadstools, shiny black

40

fungus, and things like purple mushrooms. Some of his finds even looked like proper mushrooms. Mother looked each one up carefully in her book, and said things like: 'Oh yes – but you have to boil those for ten hours,' and 'Here they are – Oh, put them down at once, Tim! They're deadly poison!'

Meanwhile, Paul and Nina were not very happy picking sloes. First their sandals fell off their feet and their feet got pricked. Then their handwoven clothes seemed too hot. Then too, they soon found that sloe-bushes have long spines – sharp ones. Then they tried tasting a sloe each and – Ugh! It was so sour that it made the inside of their mouths ragged.

Father had a better time. He fell asleep on the sunny bank, with a bunch of wild onions draped over his green striped trousers.

He never saw the strange brown face that peered at him through the hedge, and grinned a pitying grin. Shortly, the same face peered through the sloe-spines at Nina and Paul. It chuckled, but Nina and Paul did not notice it either. Mother, with her toadstool-book in front of her face, never saw or heard anything, even though the face burst into peals of wicked laughter when it looked at her. But Tim saw a crooked hand come out of a bush, with a long brown finger, beckoning. He went where it beckoned. He had a marvellous time. He found a long rope of beautiful shiny red berries. Luckily he dragged the rope to Mother before he tried to eat the berries. 'Look! I found some pretty blackberries.'

'Put them down!' Mother screamed. 'Those are bryony. They're deadly poison!'

Tim dropped the beautiful berries as if they were red-hot and hurried away, thinking Mother was very angry.

Maybe this was what made Mother decide they had picked enough of the Fruits of the Earth. She picked up her basket of toadstools, called Paul and Nina, and woke Father up. Then nobody could find Tim. They called and shouted until the woods rang.

Finally, Tim came trotting up from a quite unexpected direction. He was smiling broadly and clutching a plastic bag with something bright pink inside.

'What have you got there?' Mother said suspiciously.

'Mushroom,' Tim said proudly. 'A funny man gave it me, with trousers like Father's.'

Father was very cross from sleeping in the sun. He hustled everyone back into the car, and, by the time anyone thought to ask Tim about his funny man, Tim had forgotten. He was only very young.

When they got home, the first thing Mother did was to take the plastic bag in her finger and thumb – with a shudder, because plastic is made in factories – and throw it away. The thing Tim called a mushroom rolled out on to the Persian rug. It was quite round, bright pink, and fluffy like a baby chicken.

'It looks like the bobbles on my slippers!' Nina said. She stroked the toadstool, as she used to stroke her slippers. Everyone stroked it. It felt lovely. Mother looked it up in her toadstool-book, but it did not seem to be there. So, because she was busy trying to make sloe jam and chopping the wild onions to cook with the other toadstools, she told Paul to throw it away.

The others helped Mother. Mother was determined not to make jam with sugar, because that came from a factory. They were all busy scraping out honey-jars and trying to suggest that brown sugar was almost Natural, when Paul came back.

'I can't throw it away,' he whispered. 'It's grown to the carpet.'

It had. Nina and Tim went to look. The round pink ball had put out a firm little stalk and was now growing in the middle of the Persian rug.

'Leave it,' said Nina. 'It's so pretty.'

After that, they were even busier, leaning over the jam-pan scooping hundreds of little tiny stones out from the boiling sloes. Nobody thought about the fluffy pink toadstool, until Tim came shouting proudly: 'I got *two* mushrooms now!'

He had. There were now two round furry pink toadstool-things growing in the Persian rug.

'I think,' Father said doubtfully, 'that we ought to throw it away now, before it does that again.'

But Tim said it was *his* mushroom. Nina said it was exactly like her slippers now, and Paul said it was interesting. And Mother settled it by rushing in with another toadstool-book. 'I've found it! It doesn't say it's pink, but I'm sure this is it. It's called Lady's Slipper and I think you can eat it.'

Just then, the sloe jam boiled over, and everyone forgot about the two round pink furry toadstools. When they had wiped up all the black, burnt syrup, Paul thought to go and look at them again. There were now four round pink furry toadstools, growing in a neat square on the Persian rug. Paul was so interested that he said nothing.

Soon after that, the jam was done. They tasted it. And it was clear that a jar of honey, even mixed with a packet of brown sugar, had not done anything for the sloes. It was acutely, horribly, *uneatably* sour. They all had to clean their teeth. When she had done that, Nina went to look at the pink toadstools. There were now eight of them, almost in a ring.

'I think they double every hour,' said Paul.

'Let's look again in an hour,' said Nina.

They did, while Mother was cooking the other toadstools for supper. By that time, there were sixteen round pink furry toadstools, growing in a proper ring in the Persian rug. But they forgot them again after that, because Mother served the boiled toadstools with the chopped wild onions. Quite a number of them, despite being beaten with a hammer, were as hard to eat as the soles of their hand-made sandals. Some of the others did not seem quite as nutritious as Mother's book said they were. Everyone felt rather unwell. But the worst part of the supper was the wild onions. Father, as he chewed them – they had all got used to good, hard chewing that summer – remarked: 'Plenty of taste in these onions.'

There was indeed plenty of taste. In fact, there was too much. For the rest of the evening nobody could taste anything but wild onion. They could still taste it when they went to bed, and they went to bed rather early, all feeling a little seedy.

Meanwhile, the sixteen round, pink, furry toadstools quietly became thirty-two round, pink, furry toadstools. These thirty-two became sixty-four, and these sixty-four . . . All through the night, silently and mysteriously, the round, pink, furry toadstools doubled in number, once every hour. Soon there was no room for a ring of them. Soon . . .

When everyone came down in the morning, still tasting wild onions, the floor of the living-room was a mass of fluffy pink. Fluffy pink had grown up the walls and was just meeting in the middle of the ceiling round the light. Fluffy pink had begun to spread to the kitchen. That was when Father put his foot down.

Mother, he said, was welcome to any daft ideas she wanted. But she was to have them on her own. If she tried to make any of the rest of the family take part in her crazes, Father said, he would leave, and he would take Tim and Nina and Paul with him. And, to prove that he meant what he said, he took all three children out for the day and left Mother to get rid of the toadstools.

Mother's latest craze is playing the violin. But she does it by herself. If the rest of the family keep all the doors shut, they hardly notice it at all.

Auntie Bea's Day Out

'I shall take the children for a lovely day at the seaside tomorrow,' said Auntie Bea.

The children felt miserable. Auntie Bea was huge, with a loud voice. She had been staying with the Pearsons for a week then, and they all felt crushed and cross.

'You needn't bother to drive us, Tom,' said Auntie Bea. 'I can easily go by bus.' This was Auntie Bea's way of telling Mr Pearson he was to drive them to the seaside.

Mr Pearson looked very cheerful. 'Isn't that lucky? I have to take the car for its MOT tomorrow.'

When Auntie Bea decided to do something, she did it. She turned to Mrs Pearson. 'Well, you can help me carry things, Eileen.'

Mrs Pearson hastily discovered that she was going to the dentist.

'Then Nancy will help,' said Auntie Bea. 'Nancy's so sensible.'

'No, I'm not,' said Nancy.

'So that's all right,' said Auntie Bea. She never attended to anything the children said. 'Nancy can look after Debbie, and Simon can carry the things.'

The number of things Auntie Bea needed for a day at the seaside would have been about right if she was

46

going to climb Mount Everest. Mr Pearson helped her pile them in the hall, in twenty-two separate heaps. Auntie Bea was so afraid of losing or forgetting some of them that she wrote out twenty-two labels, each with their names and address on it, and tied them to the bundles. Meanwhile, Mrs Pearson cut up four loaves to make the number of sandwiches Auntie Bea thought they would need.

'And little jellies in yoghurt cups,' Auntie Bea said, racing into the kitchen. '*Such* a good idea!'

Mrs Pearson was so glad to be getting rid of Auntie Bea for a day that she made them two jellies each.

'I feel like a human sacrifice,' Simon said. 'How does she think I can carry all that and manage Honey as well?' Honey was due to have puppies any day now. Simon was too anxious about her to leave her behind.

Auntie Bea came downstairs shaking out a vast swimsuit. It was electric blue with shiny orange hearts all over it. Nancy blinked, and wondered what Auntie Bea would look like wearing it.

'That's pretty,' said Debbie, who loved bright colours. 'I shall make Teddy a swimsuit like that.'

'I hope it rains,' said Nancy.

Unfortunately, the next day was bright and sunny. But they missed the early bus, because of Teddy and Honey. Debbie had pinned a scarf round Teddy like a nappy, and she had written him a label too: *Deb's Ted wiv care in Emurjunsy fone Millwich 29722.*

As soon as Auntie Bea saw Teddy, she said, 'No, dear. We only take things we need today.'

Debbie's face took on its most mulish look, and the argument only ended when Auntie Bea saw Honey drooping joylessly on the end of her lead.

'You can't take him, dear. He might have his puppies at any moment!' Just as Auntie Bea never attended to children, she never attended to whether dogs were females.

That argument was only finished when Simon found he could not carry all his bundles, even without Honey.

'You'll have to leave the stove and the kettle,' said Mrs Pearson, very anxious to see them off.

'In that case, we must take plenty of boiled water!' said Auntie Bea. 'Think of the germs!'

So Simon's bundles were repacked and they set off to catch the later bus. Nancy went first with a light load of: one tartan rug, one carrier-bag of sandwiches, a first-aid box and a bundle of buckets and spades. Auntie Bea sailed behind hung about with: one folding chair, one striped umbrella, three pints of milk, a bag of sweaters, a bag of suntan cream, a packet of sandwiches, two dozen hard-boiled eggs, a complete change of Outsize clothes, three books and a radio. Debbie trotted behind that with: a bundle of towels, a beachball in a string bag and a basket full of jellies and cake, with Teddy defiantly sitting in it too. A long, long way behind came Simon. He was not sure what was in the rucksack, nor what was in his other six bundles, but he could see Thermos flasks sticking out of one and an electric torch out of another. His knees buckled under it all, and Honey kept tangling her lead round them. Honey did not seem happy.

'It will serve him right if he has his puppies in the sea,' Auntie Bea said, and counted the bundles to make sure they had remembered them all.

Nothing much happened on the bus ride, except that Honey threatened to be sick. When they got to

Millhaven, it was quite late in the morning and already very crowded.

'Crowds, germs!' said Auntie Bea, counting everything again. 'We should have caught the early bus.' She hoisted up her twelve bundles and set off happily down the steps to the sand, calling, 'Don't bother to help with all this. I can manage perfectly.'

They struggled after her down the steps and caught her up on the sand.

'Debbie,' said Auntie Bea, 'you take the umbrella. If Nancy takes the folding chair, I can manage perfectly.'

'No, I won't,' said Debbie. 'It was you brought it.'

'Why don't we stop just here?' Nancy asked.

Debbie's refusal brought out the worst in Auntie Bea. She gave a scornful look round the deck-chairs, rugs and sandcastles on the crowded beach, and called out to the man who hired the deck-chairs in her loudest, most hooting voice: 'My good man, can you direct me to somewhere less crowded?'

The deck-chair man scratched his head. 'Well, it thins out a bit up there, ma'am, but you can't go in the rocks. Tourists are not allowed on the island.'

Auntie Bea stuck up her head indignantly at being called a tourist and set off at a trot where the man pointed, hooting to the children to come along. They ploughed after her, making zigzags round the other families, who all stared, because Auntie Bea kept turning round and hooting at them. To the right were the lovely white waves of the sea, rolling, folding and breaking with a joyful smash, but Auntie Bea would not hear of stopping. Honey, on the other hand, would not walk. She had never seen the sea before. All she knew was that it was the biggest bath in the universe, and she dreaded baths. Simon had a terrible time with her.

Nancy suggested that they stopped for the donkeys, and for the swings, and for one of the ice-cream carts. But Auntie Bea just cried out 'Germs!' and scudded on. She would not stop until they had left all the people behind, and there was nothing but rocks. There was a kind of road of rocks stretching into the sea and, at the end of the road, an island. It was quite small — only big enough to hold a tuft of trees.

'The very place!' cried Auntie Bea, and went out over the rocks like Steve Ovett winning a race.

Honey, for some reason, was even more afraid of the island than the sea. Simon had to walk backwards, dragging her. When he turned round at the end, he found there was a barbed-wire fence round the island and a large notice on the gate: ISLAND ISLAND KEEP OUT.

There was no time to wonder about that. Auntie Bea was already charging through the trees. Simon dragged Honey past another notice: NO TRES-PASSERS, and yet another: TRESPASSERS WILL BE SORRY. By that time, Auntie Bea had stopped and he caught up.

'I don't think we ought to be on this island,' Nancy was saying.

'Nobody's afraid of three ignorant notices, dear,' said Auntie Bea. 'We're going to camp here.'

Everyone was too tired to protest. They threw down the bundles and thankfully tipped the sand out of their shoes. Honey lay down, panting. She looked rather ill. Auntie Bea prepared to put on her swimsuit. First she spread the rug out. Then she arranged the chair and the screen and the umbrella to make a sort of hut. Finally, she crawled mountainously in to undress.

Nancy and Debbie undressed where they were, and Simon tried to do the same. His shirt was stuck to his back by something sticky and smelling loudly of strawberry.

'I think the jellies have leaked on you,' Debbie said, and crawled over to look at the yoghurt cups in her basket. The sun had melted every one, and, in the mysterious way things happen at the seaside, every one was half full of sand. Teddy was soaked in strawberry juice. 'This is *awful*!' said Debbie, and put Teddy on the branch of a tree to dry.

'Don't grumble, dear,' Auntie Bea called out of her hut. 'We're having a *lovely* time!'

The island gave a curious shudder. It made them very uneasy.

'Auntie Bea,' said Nancy. 'I really think we ought to move.'

'Nonsense, dear,' called Auntie Bea.

At that, the island gave a bigger shudder and a heave. It felt as if they were going over a hump-bridge in a car. And everything was different.

There was a strong wind. They were all kneeling or standing on very short grass, shivering. There were no trees. Teddy was hanging in the air above Auntie Bea's hut. They could hear the sound of waves crashing all round in the distance, from which they could tell they were on another, bigger island. But they had no idea where.

Almost at once, a hot man in a beret came panting up the green slope towards them. He was wearing a brown sweater with green patches on the elbows and shoulders. 'I say!' he shouted. 'You lot can't picnic here! You're right in the middle of a gun-range there!'

51

The umbrella heaved. Auntie Bea appeared, looking larger than ever. She had her skirt round her neck like a poncho. 'Don't talk nonsense, my good man,' she said. The soldier stared at her, and at Teddy hanging over her head. He gave a sort of swallow. 'We leave here over my dead body,' said Auntie Bea, and dived back inside her hut.

'That's just what it will be –' the soldier started to say, when the island once more tried to shake them off – if that was what it was doing. There was a jerk, and they were on a small rock in the middle of a lake.

'People don't order me about,' Auntie Bea remarked from inside her hut.

There was another jerk, and they were somewhere dark, with water heaving nearby. Honey began to shiver.

'We're having a lovely day!' Auntie Bea asserted, from behind the umbrella.

The island jerked again, quite angrily, and it was freezing cold, but light enough to see by. There was frost or ice under their bare knees. The frosty space was rather small, and heaving, as if it was floating. The sea was very near, dark green, in frighteningly big waves.

'This is an iceberg,' said Nancy, with her teeth chattering. 'That's cheating.'

'How many more kinds of island are there?' shivered Simon. 'No, don't tell me. You'll put ideas in its head. Good dog, Honey.'

'Oh!' Debbie shrieked. 'Teddy's gone! I want to go home. Teddy!'

Auntie Bea, shielded from the ice by her blanket and screened from the view by her hut, called out, 'Don't spoil our lovely day by screaming, dear.'

The iceberg jerked, a bob of annoyance. They were

on ice still, but this time it was the top of a mountain. Instead of water, they were surrounded by clouds.

'Teddy!' cried Debbie.

'Lovely day,' repeated Auntie Bea.

Another jerk instantly flung them into sweltering heat, somewhere low down and steamy. Water bubbled between their toes and brown water slid past a few feet away. Honey growled and Nancy gasped. An unmistakable alligator slid by with the water.

'I agree with Debbie,' said Nancy. 'I want to go home.'

'Can't we shut Auntie Bea up?' Simon whispered. 'She keeps annoying it.'

'You'll feel better when you're in the water, dears,' Auntie Bea called out.

Nancy was still shouting, 'No!' when they were pitched somewhere cooler, crowded among bushes under a tall tree. There seemed to be a river in front of them, and park railings beyond that. A banana skin fell heavily on Simon's head. He looked up to find that the tree was full of interested monkeys. Several of them came down to inspect Auntie Bea's hut.

To Simon's amazement, a small boy was staring at them through the railings. 'Hey, Mum,' said the small boy, 'can I have a picnic on there, too?'

'I want to go home, too,' Simon said uncomfortably.

Two of the monkeys had decided that Auntie Bea's umbrella was fun. They tried to take it up the tree with them. Auntie Bea's hand appeared round the edge of it, slapping.

'Don't be so impatient, dears. I'm nearly ready.'

The monkeys had barely time to chitter angrily, before that island tossed them aside, too. Auntie Bea's hut was suddenly in the middle of a neat flowerbed.

Debbie was rolling in red geraniums. There was a great deal of noise all round, but it was not water. It sounded like traffic. Simon jumped to his feet. He was on a mound surrounded by cars and lorries. Faces were pressed against the windows of a passing bus, staring at him.

'We're on a traffic island now,' he said. 'In the middle of a roundabout.'

Nancy stood up, too. 'What will it think of next? I say, Honey's not here!'

'Ready, dears,' called Auntie Bea. She stood up out of her hut in her bathing suit. Simon was gazing round for Honey, but even he was distracted by the sight. Auntie Bea was gigantic. The flowers looked pale beside her. She was like an enormous beachball, only brighter than a beachball has any right to be. The people going by in cars could not take their eyes off her. The bus ran into the kerb. Two cars drove up on to the flowerbeds. Brakes squealed and metal clanged all round the roundabout.

Only Debbie was not distracted by the sight. She was fond of bright colours. 'This is the roundabout at the end of our road!' she said.

'Quick!' said Nancy.

'Run!' said Simon. 'Before she says anything.'

They raced down among the flowers. Behind them, Auntie Bea hooted, 'I do think cars should be banned on beaches,' and vanished from sight – which caused a further pile-up of cars.

Nancy, Simon and Debbie dodged between the cars and ran on, up their road and into their own house.

'Why are you back so soon!' asked Mrs Pearson. She did not seem to have gone to the dentist. 'Where's Auntie Bea?'

She could not understand what had happened. All

54

Debbie could think of was Teddy, last seen floating in the air over a soldier. All Simon could think of was Honey, last seen growling at an alligator. All Nancy could think of was that she was never going near another island — of any kind — as long as she lived. Neither Mr or Mrs Pearson grasped that something truly odd had happened, until the phone began to ring.

The first caller was very polite and very high up in the Army. They had Teddy, he said, on an island somewhere in Scotland. Could any of the Pearsons please reveal the secret formula that made Teddy float in the air? Was it anything to do with the strawberry juice Teddy was soaked in? When nobody could tell him what made Teddy float, the high-up man said that it certainly had military importance, and would Debbie mind if they kept Teddy for analysis? They would send a new teddy.

'I want my Ted!' Debbie shouted, but the Army said it was impossible.

The next person to phone was a Swiss Mountain Guide, who had found the beachball on top of a mountain, complete with the label giving their address. He asked if they wanted it back. They never did answer that, because a policeman called just then, looking rather grim and asking to speak to Auntie Bea. She had caused a Breach of the Peace, he said, and left her radio in the middle of Silas Street roundabout. But nobody, of course, knew where Auntie Bea was by then.

Almost straight away, there was a puzzled phonecall from Iceland. A trawler captain had found a bag of Pearson sweaters floating on an iceberg and wondered if there were any survivors from the wreck. Mr Pearson had just sorted that one out when someone telephoned all the way from South America. His English was not very good, but he seemed to be saying that the water had ruined the battery in the electric torch. But he wanted to assure them that the buckets and spades were quite safe and very useful.

'Ask about Honey,' said Simon.

But the person in South America had not seen a dog, nor even a satisfied-looking alligator.

'Where's Auntie Bea, though?' Mrs Pearson kept asking.

It was soon clear that Auntie Bea was still travelling. The Foreign Office phoned next. There was, they said, a mysterious complaint from the Russian Embassy. A basket full of jelly and sand in yoghurt cups, with the Pearsons' address on it, had somehow appeared on the conning-tower of a Russian submarine. The Russians were holding it for analysis. The Foreign Office wanted to know if they would find anything important in the yoghurt cups.

'I don't think so,' said Mrs Pearson weakly. 'They – they didn't find my sister as well, did they?'

But Auntie Bea had not been heard of. Nor had she been seen by an excited lady in Greece, who phoned next. This lady wanted the Pearsons to know that she was not so poor that she could not find two dozen hard-boiled eggs for herself, thank you. And she was throwing away the bag of clothes. They were too big for anyone on the island. She rang off before anyone could try to explain.

The American Embassy rang next. Auntie Bea's umbrella had been found in the sea off Honolulu. They wondered if Auntie Bea had been drowned. So did the Pearsons. But since the next two calls were from Sweden and Japan, it began to look as if Auntie Bea was still being jerked from island to island.

Quite late that night, the London Zoo phoned. 'It's taken us all this time to trace you,' they said, rather injured. 'The address fell off on our monkey-island. How did you come to leave your dog there, anyway? The monkeys were trying to play with the puppies.'

Mr Pearson said – a little wildly – that he could explain everything. Then he found that the Zoo wanted him to collect Honey and her six new puppies at once. They were in the Children's Zoo. Simon was greatly relieved. He went with his father to fetch Honey, and did not mind in the least when Honey was car-sick, though Mr Pearson did.

Meanwhile the others were still answering the telephone, and there was still no news of Auntie Bea. They forgot what a trial Auntie Bea had been and became worried. They had tender, troubled thoughts about where she could be. Nancy feared she was marooned on a desert island like Robinson Crusoe, all alone in her bathing suit. Debbie said she was somewhere where they spoke quite another language. Mrs Pearson wrung her hands and said she *knew* Bea was in China, under arrest.

Three days later, Auntie Bea rang up herself. 'You'll never guess, Tom!' she hooted. 'I'm in the Bahamas. I've no idea how I got here, and I've had to borrow money for the phone. You needn't bother to come and get me, Tom. I can manage.'

Mr Pearson thought of all the phone calls, and Debbie still in tears about Teddy and – very crossly – about Honey sick in his clean car. 'I'm glad you can manage, Bea,' he said. 'Come and see us when you get home.' And he rang off.

Carruthers

Carruthers was a walking-stick for beating Father with.

Elizabeth acquired Carruthers on a visit to Granny, when she was very small. Father had been exploring Granny's attic, and he had found the walking-stick there. It was knobby and black, with a silver band just below the curve of the handle. Elizabeth was screaming her head off at the time, but she heard Father telling Aunt Anne about it.

'It belonged to Uncle Bob,' said Aunt Anne.

Father frowned, the way he always did if Mother or Aunt Anne expressed an opinion. 'No,' he said. 'It was someone with a much stranger history. What *was* the name? Why is that child screaming?'

Elizabeth was screaming because she did not like dark chocolate. Granny had given Ruth and Stephanie milk chocolate, but she had given Elizabeth a large slab of black, bitter stuff – quite uneatable – on the grounds that Elizabeth was 'a big girl now'. Mother did not seem to understand when Elizabeth protested. So she screamed, and Mother and Granny tried to find out what the matter was. Mother thought Elizabeth was ill.

'You ought to be ashamed, a big girl like you!' said Granny. 'Look how good your little sisters are!'

Ruth and Stephanie were sitting side by side on the sofa, with the soles of their four shoes sticking neatly up in front of them, eating milk chocolate. They were happy. They liked milk chocolate. Elizabeth threw them a resentful look and screamed on.

'Hush, darling!' said Mother.

'I know it was Uncle Bob's stick,' said Aunt Anne.

Father frowned. 'It was not. Quiet, Elizabeth!'

'You ought to give the child a good smack and stand her in the corner,' Granny said to Mother.

'But I don't think she's well,' said Mother.

'Indulgence does no good,' said Granny. She turned to Father. 'Stephen, it does no good to spoil the child. It's –'

Father waved the walking-stick triumphantly at Aunt Anne. 'Carruthers!' he said. 'That was the name.' That was how Elizabeth learnt the stick's name.

' – just a rod to beat your own back, Stephen,' said Granny. 'You must be firm.' And that was how Elizabeth learnt what Carruthers was for.

She was still screaming. Father seized her arm and ran out of the room with her into the hall, roaring, 'How dare you make a noise! How dare you upset Granny!'

Elizabeth snatched at the walking-stick he was holding. 'Hit him, hit him!' she implored it. 'Hit him, Carruthers!'

Carruthers did not hit Father. It would have been hard to do, since Father and Elizabeth were each holding an end of him. Elizabeth was left sitting on the hall carpet, clutching the stick in one hand and the slab of uneatable chocolate in the other, while Father smoothed his hair and reknotted his tie. 'And don't come back in here again,' he said, as he went back to the living-room.

Elizabeth sat until the uneatable chocolate had gone melted and slimy. Then it occurred to her that Carruthers might like it. Experimentally, she held the slimy lump towards the hooked end of him.

Carruthers liked it. He was a bit languid and stiff – after all, he had never eaten anything in his life before – but he nuzzled willingly enough at Elizabeth's fingers. Elizabeth sat for a long time, pressing the chocolate against the place where his mouth seemed to be. It looked like a sort of dent in the end of him. Beyond that dent, further up the handle, were two more dents that seemed to be his eyes. Elizabeth thought that Carruthers kept his eyes blissfully closed, as he discovered how much he liked chocolate, but, when it was mostly gone, he did once open an eye like a little bright bead and roll it soulfully at Elizabeth. He liked her. Nobody else had ever fed him before.

'I think I shall feed you up and train you,' said Elizabeth, 'as a rod to beat Father's back.'

She was interrupted by Aunt Anne's son, who was called Stephen after Father, who came sauntering in from the garden with his bar of bitter chocolate. He had only managed to eat half of it. 'What are you doing?' he asked.

Elizabeth admired Stephen. He was over a year older that she was. 'Feeding Carruthers,' she said.

'Sticks don't eat,' said Stephen, and he demonstrated that they didn't by holding his chocolate against the end of Carruthers. Carruthers had already eaten so much that he could hardly manage another mouthful. Stephen's chocolate simply melted on him, and on Elizabeth too.

When everyone came into the hall, ready to go home, Granny exclaimed. 'Just look at that child! Just look at that stick! They'll have to be washed at once.'

'Carruthers doesn't want to be washed,' said Elizabeth.

Nevertheless, Granny took them both away and washed them severely. She nearly drowned Carruthers. Elizabeth cried heartily when Granny took him away and propped him in the corner of the landing, ready to go back to the attic. But Granny believed in being firm. She led the weeping Elizabeth out to the car. And, somehow, while everyone was standing around saying Goodbye, Carruthers got into the car. Elizabeth found him on the back seat when she got in.

After that, Mother, Ruth and Stephanie got used to Carruthers going everywhere with Elizabeth. Father did not. 'Why does that child have to take her blessed stick to ballet class!' Elizabeth heard him demanding.

'She says it's alive. She has a very vivid imagination, dear,' Mother explained.

'What twaddle!' said Father. 'She's just trying to be interesting.'

'He doesn't like you,' Elizabeth explained to Carruthers in a whisper, 'because he knows what you're for.'

Carruthers did not need to eat very often. The next time he fed, it was a fortnight later, just before bedtime. Elizabeth was sitting dismally in front of her rice-pudding from lunch. Father always insisted that everyone ate everything all up, or they had it for tea, then for supper, until it was gone. Stephanie once had the same mashed swede for two days, until Ruth and Elizabeth ate it for her out of pity. Elizabeth could only eat rice-pudding by being almost sick. So there she sat, staring at the cold white mush, when Carruthers suddenly unhooked himself from the back of her chair and fell forward into it. There was a bit of slurping, and the rice-pudding went.

61

Thereafter, Carruthers always ate rice-pudding, and occasionally swede for Stephanie too. Given a bit of luck, you could hook Carruthers into your plate while Father was not looking, and the food was gone when Father next looked.

After he had fed, in those early days, Carruthers would fall heavily asleep. When he was asleep, he was exactly like any ordinary walking-stick. Usually, he hid in the hall-stand, among the umbrellas, when he wanted to sleep, and it was no good trying to disturb him. But, as time went on, eating made Carruthers more and more lively. He slithered and clattered about the house so much, that Father kept storming upstairs bellowing, 'Elizabeth! Stop that confounded noise!' Elizabeth had to take Carruthers out into the woods above the house, so that he could get his exercise.

Stephanie and Ruth loved watching Carruthers in the wood. They and Elizabeth would sit in a row on a log, laughing and applauding. Carruthers climbed trees by winding himself up the trunk in a spiral, and then swung himself from hook to tail through the branches. 'Just like a monkey's tail, without the monkey,' as Stephanie said. When he felt specially skittish, Carruthers liked to shoot out from a tree like an arrow, and, instead of falling to the ground, he had a way of folding himself into coils and drifting to an immaculate landing on the earth by the log. Ruth always applauded this furiously. Carruthers went hopping and skipping about in delight, like a rather small pogo stick.

He was shy of other children. One day, a group of boys came to play in the wood and ran about all the trodden paths and plunged into all the bushes, shouting. Carruthers simply hooked himself to the tree he happened to be in and hung there. Nothing Elizabeth said would make him show any sign of life.

'It's lunch-time,' said Ruth. 'Come on, Stephanie, or we'll get into trouble.'

Ruth and Stephanie went. Elizabeth lingered. But the boys were still there, and Carruthers still would not budge. At last, Elizabeth was too scared of what Father would say to stay any longer. She had to leave Carruthers hanging there. She was very relieved to find him asleep in the umbrella-stand after lunch.

After that, Elizabeth took Carruthers out to the wood every day on her way to school and left him there. He always came back by himself – how, Elizabeth never knew. Carruthers would not say. He was very surly altogether about the way Elizabeth went to school without him.

'You take that other stick,' he complained in his small grunting voice.

'That's my hockey stick,' Elizabeth explained. 'It's not alive, like you. I only take it because I have to.'

Carruthers did not answer. He did not speak much at the best of times. When he did, it was mostly short sentences – most of them rather self-centred. He said, 'Don't forget *me*,' if Elizabeth was going anywhere except to school, and, 'Leave me alone,' if he was asleep in the umbrella-stand. His favourite short sentence was, 'I'm hungry.' He said that increasingly often as time went on. Elizabeth learnt to leap wide awake in the middle of the night, whenever the small grunting voice said plaintively in her ear, 'I'm *hungry*.'

'All right, all right,' she would say. 'I'll go down and get some biscuits. But you're to be quiet while I do.' She knew Carruthers was quite capable of helping himself to tomorrow's pudding or Stephanie's birthday cake, if she left him to look for food on his own. As it was, Mother noticed that biscuits were vanishing.

'Darling, you should ask if you want biscuits,' she said.

'Carruthers got hungry in the night,' Elizabeth said.

'Well, if he does it once more I shall have to tell Father,' Mother answered. She said it in an indulgent way which made Elizabeth suspect Mother believed it was really Elizabeth who got hungry. Elizabeth tried to make Carruthers tell Mother it was him. But Carruthers only drooped his hooked head shyly and kept his eyes tight shut until Mother had gone.

One way and another, as the years went by, there were a number of ways in which Carruthers annoyed Elizabeth. His appetite was one. Another was that he never, ever, despite all the good food and exercise he had, made any move to hit Father. Another was that Carruthers liked ballet.

Elizabeth hated ballet lessons worse than she hated rice-pudding. Ballet was a weekly torture to her. She was clumsy, she could not keep in time with the music, and the ballet positions made her arms and legs ache. The ballet teacher thought she was stupid, and said so. Mother looked sad and anxious. The worst of it was that Ruth and Stephanie were good at ballet. Ruth was very good. Stephanie did not love dancing the way Ruth did, but she was strong, limber and willing, and she was soon much better at it than Elizabeth. Ruth and Stephanie both looked trim and lissom in pink shoes and black leotards. Elizabeth looked a fright. Her calves bulged above the pink shoes, her stomach bulged out of the leotard, and, when she put on the pink fluffy jacket you wore to keep warm, it made her look like an apewoman.

'You look like an apewoman,' Ruth said, and laughed. This did not help Elizabeth to love ballet any better.

Carruthers loved ballet. He picked up a great deal while he was propped in the corner of the dance-room watching Elizabeth flop and struggle about on the polished floor. At night, he hooked himself to the end of Elizabeth's bed and tried to do barre-exercises. It is not easy to do ballet if you have no arms and legs, but this did not deter Carruthers. He stretched straight out from the bed-rail to do the arm-positions with his tail end. Then he collapsed gracefully into a plié, rose, and sank again. After that, he let go of the bed and went hopping round the room in one-legged jetés, pirouettes and arabesques. He was very ingenious about them. He had picked up the music Elizabeth danced to, along with the steps, and he would hum Handel's Water Music in his tinny growl as he capered. Elizabeth squealed with laughter, which very often had her in trouble with Father.

Then came the dreadful day when Ruth won a scholarship to a London academy to train as a dancer. Father was delighted, but it occurred to him to wonder why Elizabeth and Stephanie had not won scholarships too. He discovered that Elizabeth was two grades behind even Stephanie. Elizabeth felt as if a volcano had erupted under her.

When Father had smoothed his hair and straightened his tie and gone away, Mother came to find Elizabeth, who was in her bedroom, sullenly hugging Carruthers.

'Darling,' Mother said, with her sad and anxious look, 'you must try harder at ballet. Girls must learn to be graceful.'

'I hate ballet,' Elizabeth said. 'You know I do. And I'm not graceful, so why should I learn to be?'

'Father has very strong opinions – ' Mother began.

'Bother and blast Father's opinions!' Elizabeth shrieked. 'What about *your* opinions? You know I'm bad at ballet, but you're too feeble to *say*!' Mother looked so hurt and shocked, that Elizabeth said hastily: 'Carruthers says you're feeble.'

Mother went to the door, more shocked than ever. 'Darling, I can't stay and listen to nonsense.'

'And Carruthers says Father's a – a bloodthirsty tyrant!' Elizabeth bawled at the closing door.

As the door shut behind Mother, Carruthers struggled out of Elizabeth's arms and stood upright in front of her, hopping gently up and down in his indignation. 'I never said that!' he said. 'Tell her I never said it.'

'No, I shan't,' said Elizabeth. 'It's true.'

'It may be true, but I never said it,' Carruthers insisted.

'You only didn't say it because you like ballet,' Elizabeth retorted. 'When are you going to hit Father?'

Carruthers squirmed sulkily. 'All in good time.'

'Soon,' said Elizabeth.

'Why?' said Carruthers.

'Because he deserves it,' said Elizabeth.

They separated, both in furious sulks. Carruthers stayed in the umbrella-stand, and Elizabeth left him there. He would not speak to her, or eat, and he never seemed to move. But he was always in the car when it was time to go to ballet lesson. Elizabeth left him in it. Twice, Stephanie ran after her with him, and once even Ruth, who was rather nervous of him, carried him cautiously into the dance-room, saying, 'You left Carruthers in the car, Elizabeth.' Elizabeth sighed. But she realized it was no good trying to keep

Carruthers away from ballet and let him stand in the corner as usual after that.

This was a little before Easter. Ruth was to go to her Academy in the Autumn. Meanwhile, Aunt Anne had to go abroad and Stephen came to live with them. He was to have gone to Granny, but Granny telephoned Father to say she could not cope, and Father said they would have Stephen instead. He could have Elizabeth's room, and Elizabeth could move in with Ruth and Stephanie, as Ruth was going away before long.

Much as Elizabeth disliked this arrangement, Ruth liked it even less. Ruth and Stephanie had shared a room since they were both small. Ruth had developed a series of masterly arrangements with Stephanie. They were all very complicated and they all amounted to the same thing: Ruth lay on her bed and gave orders while Stephanie ran and did things. When Elizabeth moved in, Ruth rightly feared that this golden time was over. Sure enough, Elizabeth saw through the arrangements at once.

'Don't be such a lazybones, Ruth,' she kept saying. 'Why should Stephanie do it?'

Ruth began to lose her temper. Stephanie was uncomfortable too. It was not what she was used to.

'Honestly, Ruth, you are lazy!' Elizabeth said for the tenth time.

Ruth pressed her lips together. Her way of losing her temper was to go icy calm and say the nastiest thing she possibly could. She took a long breath. For a moment, calm as she was, she wondered if she dared say it. 'I − I don't believe in Carruthers,' she said.

'You what?' said Elizabeth.

'I don't,' said Ruth, 'believe in Carruthers.'

'He's only a stick,' Stephanie added loyally.

Elizabeth felt extremely anxious. Ever since their quarrel, Carruthers had indeed seemed almost like an ordinary stick. Elizabeth was afraid he was dead, until she remembered the way he kept turning up at ballet. That so relieved her that she said, 'Have it your own ways,' and hurried downstairs to fetch Carruthers from the hall.

Her sisters stared at one another. 'Do you think she's all right?' Stephanie asked anxiously.

'She's grown out of Carruthers, that's all.' Ruth said. She did not really believe it, but she knew she had to keep Stephanie's respect, or Stephanie would never run errands for her again.

'Carruthers,' Elizabeth said to the unresponsive, stick-like Carruthers, as she carried him upstairs. 'Carruthers, would you like some chocolate?' Even that did not move Carruthers. Elizabeth came back into the room looking so miserable that Ruth relented. Ruth was going away to learn to be a ballerina, after all. She could afford to be kind. Besides, she thought she had hit on a way to make peace with Elizabeth and still keep Stephanie's respect.

'Never mind, Elizabeth,' Ruth said. 'You're growing up fearfully pretty, so it doesn't matter.'

This did not comfort Elizabeth. Nor did it keep Stephanie respectful. 'Ahah!' Stephanie cried out, curled up like a gnome on her pillow. 'When Ruth says that, you can believe it. Ruth's a real girl. She really works at it.'

'You're both horrible,' said Ruth. 'Worse than Stephen.'

Stephen turned out to have grown into a very boyish boy. He played with cars, guns and electric trains. He made friends with all the boys who swarmed through the bushes in the wood. They came to call on him, so, for the first time, the house filled with boys.

'Rude, rough lot!' Ruth said disgustedly.

But Elizabeth discovered that the games boys played were fun. She liked guns, Cops and Robbers, and pelting about shouting. It was much more interesting to climb trees in the wood than to sit decorously on a log watching Carruthers. She admired Stephen. Whenever he let her, she followed him about and tried to join in the games.

'Elizabeth, I forbid you to get dirty,' said Father.

'Darling, you mustn't act so rough,' said Mother.

At first, Stephen was not at all pleased to have a girl tagging about after him. 'We don't want you,' he said to Elizabeth in the hall one morning. His friend Dave had called for him, and they were going to play parachutes in the wood.

'Why not?' asked Elizabeth.

'Because you're forbidden to get dirty,' Stephen said, as he went out through the front door.

'I don't want to come anyway,' Elizabeth shouted after him. 'I've got Carruthers.'

'That stupid old stick!' Stephen called back. The front door slammed.

Carruthers was propped lifelessly in the umbrella-stand. '*He* gets dirty,' Elizabeth said to him indignantly.

The front door opened again. Stephen and Dave appeared. 'I've changed my mind,' Stephen said. Elizabeth beamed, in spite of having Carruthers.

'Er – hm,' said Dave.

Stephen said swiftly, 'Dave here wants you to be his girl-friend, Elizabeth. Tell him I've already booked you.' Elizabeth stared rather, and then opened her mouth to say that she did not like either of them nearly enough. 'Well, that's settled then,' Stephen said airily. 'Come along, Elizabeth.'

Being Stephen's girlfriend was rather like being Stephanie under Ruth's arrangements, Elizabeth discovered. It seemed to mean that she was allowed to carry Stephen's sweater, to sit at the bottom of a tree to catch him in case he fell, to be squaw – an almost lifeless role – when they played Indians, and to sit for cramped hours switching electric trains when she was told. It also seemed to mean that Stephen was allowed to talk to her in the same bullying way Father used to Mother and Aunt Anne, and to frown whenever Elizabeth made any kind of suggestion. There did not seem to be any advantages to the post at all. After two days, Elizabeth was wishing she knew how to stop being Stephen's girlfriend. But the post seemed to be a permanent one.

She was almost glad when Father started his Easter holidays and took Stephen over – except that she was also immeasurably indignant. Father was scarcely strict with Stephen at all, and he positively encouraged him to get dirty. He took him to fly a kite and to the Zoo and on a cycle ride. None of the girls were taken. Ruth seemed to think it was all right, because Stephen was a boy. Elizabeth thought it was unfair. And so, it seemed, did Stephanie.

'Mother,' Stephanie said, 'why is Father nicer to Stephen than to us?'

'Your Father's always wanted a boy,' said Mother. 'His own flesh and blood.' Elizabeth could hardly hear her for the sounds of hammering and sawing in the garage, where Father and Stephen were now making a table together.

'So am I his own flesh and blood,' Stephanie said

loudly, above the banging. 'And I can cycle and get dirty. And,' she added, as there came a softer thump and a screech from Stephen, 'I can knock in nails without hitting my thumb. Why aren't I allowed to?'

'It's not suitable for girls – ' Mother began.

'Good Lord!' said Stephanie.

'Stephanie! Don't swear!' said Mother.

'I wasn't. I only said Good Lord. You should hear some of the things the other girls say,' said Stephanie. 'Give me one good reason why it's not suitable.'

Mother got out of that by being hurt. 'Stephanie, how could you speak to me like that?' She left the room, still looking hurt.

'Did you ever know anyone so old-fashioned as our parents?' Stephanie asked Elizabeth. 'There's a girl at school calls her father Fishface. Imagine what Father or Mother would say if I called Father that – or even if I called him Dad. What can we do about them?'

'I don't know,' said Elizabeth. Privately, she thought of Carruthers. She went out of the house and met Stephen as he came out of the garage sucking his finger. 'Are you enjoying it with Father?' she asked.

Stephen rolled his eyes up. 'Holy fishcake! But,' he added, 'you wouldn't understand.'

Elizabeth knew she did not understand. All she knew was that, now Stephanie had pointed out the kind of people Mother and Father were, she felt shocked – and the fact that she felt shocked made her feel as if she were sitting in a very small cage, with no room to unbend her knees, which, in turn, made her feel angry. She tried to describe her feelings to the stiff, unresponsive Carruthers in the middle of the night. 'It's like being squeezed into the wrong shape,' she said. 'Stephanie feels the same. I'm not sure about

Ruth, but I don't think Stephen enjoys it any more than we do. But I think it would all come right if you hit Father. Couldn't you forgive me now and start hitting him? Once a day, just for a start.'

To her pleasure, Carruthers stirred sleepily. 'I'm hungry,' he said, in the old plaintive grunt. 'Terribly hungry.'

'Thank goodness for that!' said Elizabeth. 'I'll get some biscuits. What's been wrong with you?'

'I was sleepy,' said Carruthers.

Elizabeth slipped out of bed and started downstairs, into the queer orange gloom the street lights cast in the hall. But Carruthers was evidently too hungry to wait. She saw him slither along the bannisters beside her and hop ahead of her into the kitchen. Elizabeth hurried after him. Carruthers was in the larder somewhere by the time she got there. She could hear him clattering on one of the higher shelves.

'There's nothing but tins up here,' said the plaintive, grunting voice.

'The biscuits are down here,' Elizabeth whispered. 'Stop making such a noise.'

There was a scuffling, and a crunch of tinfoil. Carruthers said, 'Oh! Chocolate eggs!'

'Those are for Easter!' Elizabeth whispered frantically. 'Come *down*.'

'In a minute,' said Carruthers, munching and rustling.

The light in the larder snapped on. Rows of tins and jams leapt into sight. A very squeaky voice, which Elizabeth just recognized as Stephen's, said: 'Oh. It's only you. What are you doing?'

'Carruthers was hungry,' Elizabeth explained. Carruthers was still rustling and munching up on the shelf.

'Pull the other leg,' said Stephen. 'Sticks can't eat.' He came into the larder and stared up at the rustling.

A tin of plums promptly fell heavily on his bare foot. Stephen hopped about, yelling. Another tin fell on him, and another. Elizabeth could glimpse Carruther's hooked face peering down from the shelf, taking aim. Stephen put his arms over his head and ran out of the larder. He ran straight into Father, coming the other way.

'What is going on?' Father roared.

Carruthers prudently pushed himself off the shelf with the last tin and clattered to the floor like an ordinary walking stick. Unfortunately, he brought a torn Easter egg wrapping down with him.

'I thought it was a burglar, Uncle Stephen,' Stephen said.

'So did I,' Elizabeth said unconvincingly.

Father naturally came to the conclusion that Elizabeth had been using Carruthers to hook down Easter eggs. The trouble was terrible. Elizabeth spent Easter in disgrace and without an Easter egg.

'Why did you hit Stephen and not Father?' she asked Carruthers.

'Stephen called me a stick,' Carruthers said sulkily.

After that, Elizabeth could not get another word out of him. Most of the time, there was no way of knowing he was anything other than a real stick. Yet night after night, for the whole of the next month, the larder was raided. Biscuits, cakes and puddings went. Father blamed Elizabeth every time. Stephen found it very funny. 'Carruthers hungry again?' he asked every morning.

Elizabeth wondered why she had ever liked Stephen. If she could have thought of a way of stopping being his girlfriend, she would have stopped it that moment.

But it did no good to tell Stephen she did not want to be his girlfriend. He would say, 'All right,' as if he agreed, and then, half an hour later, he would be saying, 'Elizabeth, just come along and switch my points for me,' or 'Elizabeth, I need you to hold my coat in the wood.' It was if she had never said anything at all.

What with this, and with getting up every morning to be blamed for what Carruthers ate in the night, Elizabeth began to feel as if the cage she had imagined was getting smaller and smaller, until she could hardly breathe. She was quite sure that, if only Carruthers could be made to hit Father, everything would be all right again. 'It's like that story of the old woman and the pig,' she explained to Carruthers – who may or may not have been listening. 'Fire fire, burn stick; stick stick, beat pig – and then they all went home. You just hit Father to show him who's master, and Father will turn on Stephen, and Mother will tell Father he's a tyrant, and we'll all be able to get dirty and climb trees and so on.'

Carruthers gave no sign of hearing, but his appetite was unabated. Elizabeth began training herself to wake in the night and catch Carruthers in the larder again. She was fairly sure that if she could only catch him red-handed, she would be able to bully him into hitting Father at last. But most nights she just slept. Some nights she woke up, only to find Carruthers hooked on to the end of her bed, apparently as good as gold – except that more food was gone in the morning.

Then, one night, she was suddenly wide awake. She heard Carruthers unhook himself from her bed and go softly thumping downstairs.

Here's where I catch you, my lad! Elizabeth

thought. She flung back her bedclothes and crept after Carruthers, into the dim orange light from the street lights. On the stairs, she listened hard. There was a faint chink and rattle from the living-room, as if Carruthers had gone after the nuts and olives Mother kept to offer visitors. But, while Elizabeth was turning that way, she heard a furtive crunkling and rustling from the kitchen too. Surely Carruthers could not be in two places at once?

By that time her eyes had grown used to the orange light. She saw Carruthers lying stretched out on the hall carpet. The middle of him seemed to be bulging.

Elizabeth forgot about the noises. She fell on her knees beside him, 'Carruthers! What's the matter?' she whispered. 'Are you ill?'

Carruthers did not answer. He was bulging from the silver collar below his hook to the ferrule at his tail, heaving, and swelling to two or three times his normal width. Though Elizabeth was sure it was only the result of greed, tears ran down her face. She wondered what sort of doctor you took a sick stick to.

The noises from the living-room became more definite. There were quiet footsteps, and the sound of things being moved. Elizabeth shot the swelling, heaving Carruthers a helpless look and crawled over to the living-room door.

It was a real burglar. A wide-shouldered, strong-looking young man was packing Father's tape-recorder into a suitcase. He already had the radio. He was taking down the silver golf-cups when Elizabeth backed away and turned to Carruthers again. Just as she turned, Carruthers stopped swelling and burst, with a sharp *crack*. The noise from the living-room stopped. So did the noises from the kitchen. Elizabeth knelt in the hall, between

75

what were certainly two burglars, and stared at Carruthers.

The split in Carruthers grew wider. Something that seemed to be a gauzy green colour bulged from the split and might have been struggling to get out. A second later, the struggling was definite. The filmy green something heaved, shoved, and finally pushed the dead halves of the stick apart and climbed out on the carpet. Elizabeth gasped. Whatever it was, it was impossibly beautiful. It had long curled antennae. Its back legs were long and thin – a little like a grasshopper's – and it seemed to have long thin arms too. It had a small piquant face, with little slanting eyes which caught the orange light and glowed blue-green beneath the antennae. Its body was draped and covered in beautiful shimmering diaphanous green, which might have been multitudes of long wings – or might have been something quite different. The creature rested, quivering, for a second or so. Then it rose on its long green legs and performed a slow, airy arabesque. Elizabeth smiled. It was Carruthers all right.

The living-room burglar still had not moved, but she could hear him breathing. It occurred to Elizabeth that, if he knew she was in the hall, he might run away and leave her in peace with Carruthers. So she said out loud:

'You were a chrysalis!'

There was no sound from either burglar, but the new gauzy Carruthers turned its little face and long, nodding antennae towards her. For one miserable minute, Elizabeth thought it could not speak. But it must have been just finding out how. 'That's right,' it said. The new voice was a good deal more silvery than

76

the old one. 'I think I've been a chrysalis for the last month.'

'Then how did you rob the larder then?' asked Elizabeth.

'For the Easter egg, you mean?' asked the creature.

'No,' said Elizabeth. 'All the other times.'

'I don't think I did,' said Carruthers. 'Being a chrysalis is like being asleep. But don't I look beautiful now I'm hatched?' It twirled slowly and elegantly along by the foot of the stairs. The gauzy draperies fluttered. Elizabeth could not but agree that it was the most exquisite being. 'I think,' said Carruthers, meditatively sinking into curtsey, 'that I need to go away now and find a mate. I have to lay some eggs. Goodbye.'

'No!' said Elizabeth. At least she had an excuse to keep Carruthers close at hand – two of them. 'Don't go yet. There's a burglar in the living-room and a burglar in the kitchen.' There were startled rustles from both places. 'You've got to stay and help me catch them.'

Carruthers gave a little fluttering jump. 'Oh, I couldn't! Besides, I must be quite the most valuable thing in the house. Just phone the police.'

Elizabeth crawled over to the phone, reflecting that Carruthers was probably quite right about his – her, that is – value. It was rather stupid of him – her, that is – to let the burglars know. The silence behind the living-room door sounded like a distinctly interested one.

Elizabeth picked up the phone. Even before she dialled 999, she knew it was dead. The burglars had been thorough. She was almost frightened for the first time. Carruthers was now fluttering slowly across the hall. Some of the gauzy drapery was beginning to act like wings. Elizabeth took hold of him — her, that is — by a transparent flowing edge. 'Ow!' said Carruthers.

Elizabeth let go and whispered: 'Keep talking, as if you were both of us. I'll fetch Father.'

'You don't still want me to hit him, do you?' Carruthers asked loudly.

Elizabeth shook her head frantically at him — her — and crawled for the stairs. Carruthers took the point and said, 'You dance exquisitely,' and danced exquisitely. 'Yes, I do, don't I?' she replied. 'You fly wonderfully. Indeed I do, but, wouldn't you say, my antennae are perhaps a trifle too long?' she asked. 'Not at all,' she answered. 'Oh, thank you,' she replied. 'You must keep telling me things like that. I'm a poor ignorant weak thing, only just hatched. But,' she told herself, 'beautiful. Yes, indeed,' she answered, losing her place in the conversation a little, 'a beautiful unearthly being, fragile and lovely . . . '

The silvery voice faded out of Elizabeth's hearing as she burst open her parents' bedroom door. 'Father! There are two burglars downstairs. One's got the radio and the golf-cups and cut off the telephone!'

'Eh?' Father sat up in bed, and seemed to understand at once. 'Be down directly. Go and call Stephen and then stay safely in your bedroom.'

Elizabeth sped to her own old room. It was empty. Stephen must have heard the burglars and gone down already. There was no sign of Father coming. But downstairs Carruthers was suddenly making a great deal of noise. Elizabeth pelted for the stairs. The door of the room she shared opened.

'What is it?' Ruth hissed.

'Burglars,' said Elizabeth.

'I thought so,' Stephanie said from behind Ruth. 'Who's shouting?'

'Carruthers,' gasped Elizabeth, and galloped downstairs.

The burglar from the living-room was out in the hall. She recognized him by his wide shoulders. He had heard what Carruthers said about her value. In the dim light, his gloved hands were snatching at the green filmy draperies, while Carruthers, to Elizabeth's admiration, was circling and swooping and fluttering, just out of reach, like an enormous moth. 'You can't catch me!' Carruthers shouted. 'You can't catch me!'

'Silly thing,' said Elizabeth. 'You'll get hurt.' She snatched up what was left of the walking-stick, but was not sure what to do after that.

'Whoopee!' screamed Carruthers, swooping across the hall. 'Beautiful me!'

The burglar dived after her. Elizabeth stuck her foot out. The burglar tripped over it and fell on his face – the oddest part of the whole thing, Elizabeth thought afterwards, was that she never saw his face at all. Carruthers wheeled briskly and planed down to land on the burglar's neck. After that, it seemed to be all over.

'Hands up!' Ruth said.

'Is he dead?' asked Stephanie. They were both on the stairs with Stephen's toy guns. They seemed disappointed to have missed killing the burglar themselves.

Elizabeth cautiously poked at the burglar with her toe. He did not move.

'He's just unconscious,' Carruthers said, standing up on the burglar's back and settling her fluttering gauzeries. 'I seem,' she said modestly, 'to have a sting in my – er – tail. I expect it's to paralyse my prey. Unless,' she added thoughtfully, 'it's my mate I should paralyse. No doubt I shall find out.'

'That's never Carruthers!' said Stephanie.

'I take it back,' Ruth said handsomely, 'about him being only a stick.'

'Yes, aren't I beautiful?' Carruthers said, with feeling.

'Give me a gun,' said Elizabeth. 'There's another burglar in the kitchen.'

'No, there isn't,' Stephen said, rather wobbly and cautious. They all turned to the kitchen door. Stephen switched the hall light on and stood sheepishly in his pyjamas. He had a slice of cake – most of a cake, in fact – in one hand, and one cheek bulged. 'Burglar under control?' he asked airily.

Elizabeth looked at him with the deepest contempt. Not only had he kept hidden in the kitchen rather than face the burglar, but, for a whole month, he had let her take the blame for robbing the larder. 'You're not my boyfriend any longer,' she said. She knew she would only have to say it once.

Father came hurrying downstairs, fully dressed and knotting his tie. 'I told you girls to stay in safety,' he said.

Elizabeth looked up at him and found she felt differently about Father too. It was not Stephen's kind of cowardice which had made Father arrive just too late: it was because he could not face even a burglar without proper clothes on. Father lived by rules – narrow rules. Elizabeth did not feel afraid of him any more. Nor did she want Carruthers to hit Father. It did not matter enough. And she said to herself, with the most enormous feeling of relief, 'Thank goodness! I needn't do ballet any more!'

Typically, Father ignored the toy guns Ruth and Stephanie were holding and looked at Stephen, and then at the prone burglar. 'Nice work, Stephen,' he said.

Before Stephen could swallow enough cake to look brave but modest, Ruth and Stephanie said in chorus, 'It wasn't him. It was Elizabeth.'

Elizabeth avoided Father's astonished eye and looked round for Carruthers. She wanted Father to know it was really Carruthers. But the hall was bright and empty. She's flown away, Elizabeth thought miserably.

Then a filmy shadow glided in front of the hall light. A gauzy something flittered at Elizabeth's cheek. Elizabeth realized that it had been a trick of the orange street lights which had made Carruthers look green. In the bright electric light she was all but invisible.

'Goodbye,' whispered Carruthers. 'I'll be back when I've laid some eggs.'

No One

One morning in the year 2084, the Right Honourable Mrs Barbara Scantion MP was talking to a friend in the House of Commons. 'Yes, it's school holidays,' she was saying. 'My husband's in Madrid. We got a foreign girl to look after Edward, but Edward's just rung up to say she's walked out again. That's the second time this week!'

'Does that mean no one's looking after Edward?' the friend asked.

'Yes. No one's looking after Edward,' Mrs Scantion said. She laughed.

A fly-on-the-wall bug recorded this conversation and it was duly passed on to the Anti-European Organisation, which wished to make use of Mrs Scantion. Unfortunately, it was entirely misunderstood.

No One was a robot – though Edward called him Nuth, short for Nothing. He was No. One in Knight Bros's special new series of White Knights, which meant he was fitted with every latest device in robotics, including a quasi-permanent power pac, long-distance radio and self-programming. He had an AT brain (meaning Advanced Type). His silver skin would only melt at extreme high temperatures, and, what was probably more useful, he could feel with his silver fingers. His pink eyes could see in the dark. In fact, he could see anything which was not actually invisible. He was programmed both to obey orders and think for himself. He was brand-new. He cost a bomb (Mr Scantion was very, very rich). And he knew he was utterly useless.

He got both his names because the Scantions looked up from reading, in the thick booklet which had come with him, that he was No. One in the White Knight Series. And the robot was not there. The passage leading to the garage door was empty. Since they had all seen the lorry drive up and deliver the big crate labelled FRAGILE THIS END UP, and since Mr Scantion had signed the delivery note with the robot unpacked and standing beside him in the garage, this puzzled everyone extremely.

It was quite simple. The moment Mr Scantion went through the door to the house, something slammed the door shut and left the garage in darkness. The robot could see another pair of large robot eyes not far away. He thought he was in a store-place for robots and was meant to stay there.

'Can you tell me if I should stay here?' he asked the other robot politely. It was a car of some kind, he could see.

Its voice seemed to be made from grinding cogwheels together. 'Think for yourself,' it grunted unhelpfully.

'Yes, but I am new,' the robot explained. 'I am a household robot, so I assume I should be in a house. But the door is shut. Why is that?'

The car gave a hydraulic sort of sigh. 'Someone shut it of course! Wirenose! If you go close to it, the circuit will cause it to open again. That's how the softbodies do it.'

'Thank you. What are softbodies?' asked the robot.

'Humans,' grunted the car. 'People. Folk. Owners.' And as the robot walked towards the door, it snarled at him, in a perfect crash of cogs. 'Learn to *think*, blobface! Or get scrapped!'

The lorry driver's mate had said that too, in the same disgusted way. The robot stepped through the door when it opened, wondering if there was something more to thinking than he had in his programmes. There were four humans (softbodies?) in the passage beyond, one of them unnaturally small, all with the lower hole in their faces pulled into an O.

'Nothing!' said Betty the foreign girl, whose English was always a stage behind the facts.

The robot advanced towards them on soundless spongy feet. 'Think,' he said. 'Consider, judge, believe, or ponder.'

To his confusion, Betty screamed and ran away, and the rest fell about laughing. Mr Scantion said, 'No need to think. Your name's No One.'

'Nothing's better,' Edward said, but this joke was not attended to.

People very seldom attended to what Edward said. This confused No One, because he was told straight away that his main job was to take care of Edward. Betty the foreign girl was considered unreliable. She broke down all the time. When she did, she sobbed that she was 'not happy!' and then put things in a blue suitcase and went away down the drive. Presumably she went to get serviced, because she always came back about twelve hours later. It became No One's job to release the switches on the gate to let Betty out, and then release them again when she came back. It was a special Security Gate, designed to keep Edward safe.

Edward was obviously very precious. No One was told that Edward was going to inherit some things called 'the firm' and 'responsibilities' later on. No One ran through the dictionary programme and discovered that 'firm' meant the same as 'hard, difficult'. This must be why Edward always went white when these things were talked about. It was a sign of slight overload, the same sort of thing that made No One's eyes pulse. Edward was being programmed, very slowly, in all sorts of hard things like manners and playing the piano. No One knew how that felt – and it had only taken six months to programme him: Edward was going to take years. He realized that Edward was very expensive indeed and treated him with great respect.

But he was confused. None of his programmes quite fitted things as they were. This was Knight Bros's fault. When Mr Scantion had ordered a household robot for Fawley Manor, someone in the office looked at a photo of the Manor and saw it was a large old house. They programmed No One for a large old house, not realising that Fawley Manor had been modernized throughout inside. The only old thing left was the stairs. The walls were energized screens and the furniture was energized foam blocks, all of which could be moved at the touch of a button, controlled by a robot fixture in the cellar. The kitchen was a mass of machinery. No One's eyes pulsed when he saw it. But Mrs Scantion had told him to cook supper because she was sick of autofood, so he located the freezer and opened it.

The freezer hummed frosty air complacently round No One. It was full of square grey frozen packets which all looked exactly alike. There was no way of telling carrots from éclairs, or beetroot from blackberries. 'You'll have to melt everything to find out what it is,' the freezer hummed.

'That would take too long,' said No One. He held up a grey packet. 'What is this?'

'Chicken drumsticks,' hummed the freezer.

'And this?' asked No One, holding up another packet.

'I've forgotten,' said the freezer. 'You won't do it that way. My self-melt will come on if you keep me open much longer.'

No One picked a bundle of grey packets out at random and shut the freezer. He put them in hot water in one of the sinks to thaw. While he was doing that, coffee beans began pouring out of a hopper in the opposite wall. No One went over to the hopper. 'Why are you doing that?' he asked.

'Making-use-of-a-faulty-circuit-to-annoy-you,' rattled the hopper. 'Boo!' And coffee beans piled on the work surface.

No One tried to locate the faulty circuit. There was a gargling behind him. Even moving at superspeed, No One was not quick enough to stop the waste-disposal in the sink from eating every one of the grey packets, and he nearly lost a finger trying to. 'Glumph,' said the waste-disposal, satisfied. As No One went to the freezer for another set of grey packets, he distinctly heard something scuttering and scrambling out of his way. But there was nothing there. Whatever it was continued to scutter and scramble from then on, confusing No One thoroughly. Since it did not seem to be there, he tried to ignore it. He stripped the plastic off the grey food and put it in the roasting oven. The autocook and the microwave at once flashed red lights at him.

'We're supposed to do that!' they said.

'I am supposed to cook by hand,' No One told them. He turned the oven on. Nothing happened. 'What is wrong with you?' No One asked it.

'I've come out in sympathy,' said the oven. 'My timer is set wrong.'

No One made the oven work and tried to set the table as his programme told him. But all the knives and forks were in the dishwasher and the dishwasher would not open. 'Drying, drying!' it said when No One tried its door. Meanwhile, coffee beans continued to pour out of the hopper. By now they were all over the floor. No One's spongy robot feet suddenly turned into skates. He careered across the kitchen area and sat down with a crash among the chairs in the dining area. There he was forced to sit for a while, checking his circuits. While he sat, the scuttering thing scrambled about under the table tittering. It almost could have been laughing. Nothing in No One's microchips had prepared him for any of this. In order to prevent extreme overload, he had to get up and go away for a while.

He came across Edward at the other end of the house, plonking away at a very simple programme on the piano. Edward stopped rather readily when he saw No One. 'Hallo, Nuth. How are you getting on?'

'I do not understand,' No One said, 'why the large humans do not attend to you or why you are so small. You seem much better programmed than me already. I shall have to be scrapped. My programmes do not fit this house.'

Edward pushed the button that spun the piano stool round and looked up at No One. No One's eyes were pulsing from pink to white. 'Poor Nuth!' he said. 'But you're self-reprogramming, aren't you? That's

87

like a human getting used to things. Are you programmed to play the piano!'

'Yes,' said No One.

A gleeful smile came into Edward's face. 'Then let's make a bargain. You do my piano practice and I'll help you reprogramme. OK?'

A bargain is not an order. No One decided it was better. His eyes stopped pulsing and he sat down at the piano. He played without having to learn how, and Edward corrected him by asking him to play slower, with random wrong notes. Both of them got something, No One realized, because, when the piano was finished with, Edward went to the kitchen area with him, where he stopped the hopper by turning off all the machinery on that side and then showed No One the suction-cleaner that cleaned the floor just by pressing a switch. Then he kicked the dishwasher and made it give up the knives and forks and plates so that No One could set the table. And he went on helping No One during supper. That was a disaster, thanks to the freezer. No One found he was serving curried prawns with bread-and-butter pudding, followed by beetroot and molten peppermint ice-cream.

'But he doesn't eat so he doesn't know!' Edward explained, while No One stood abjectly waiting to be scrapped. 'He'll know better next time.'

Betty did not agree. It was this supper that made her pack her suitcase and leave for the first time. But Mr and Mrs Scantion listened to Edward for once and No One was not even sent away for reprogramming.

'You should have used the autocooker,' Edward said to him afterwards. 'But you can't disobey an order, can you? Another time, Nuth, you're to get round it by asking me to do it.'

So a bargain was a way of getting round orders too.

88

No One felt he was learning. But not learning fast enough. Betty came back the next morning, but it was No One's fault that she left for the third time, the morning Mr Scantion went to Madrid. (The time in between was Edward's fault. He hung a hairy plastic spider in Betty's shower.) The third time, it was No One's mousetraps.

These were to catch the scuttering, tittering thing. Robots do not have nerves, of course, but if they had, this thing would have got on No One's. It seemed to follow him about, and he was certain it laughed at his mistakes. He asked Edward what it might be. Edward said it was a mouse probably. No One spent half of one night thinking about this. Since robots do not sleep, No One usually spent the nights sitting on the stairs going through his programmes and finding out where they did not match things as they were. One of his programmes was called Miscellaneous Wisdom. It did not seem to match anything. It told him that fools rush in where angels fear to tread and to answer these fools according to their folly, that many hands make light work, but too many cooks spoil the broth. But one of the things it said was, 'If you build a better mousetrap, the world will beat a path to your door.' No One considered this. He considered the scuttering thing. From the sounds it made, his acute robot hearing deduced that it was half the size of Edward. That would take a big trap.

So, for the second half of that night, No One built mousetraps, bigger and better mousetraps, out of things he found in the roof storage-space. He made forty-two, all different, and spread them around the house in all the places he knew the scuttering thing went. He was a little troubled that the world might shortly roll over on itself and beat a path through the garden, but it seemed to him that, since there was a good front drive already, the world would not feel any need to make a path as well. He did *not* put a mousetrap outside Betty's room. But, while he was still waiting to see if he had bent the world out of shape, there were terrible screams from Betty, and there she was, tangled in thirteen wire coat-hangers and the weights from an old clock.

'I am to die with this tin man!' Betty screamed.

No One was sure that someone had moved that mousetrap. He explained this to Mr Scantion, who simply ordered him to remove all forty-two traps and not to do it again. No One had moved thirty-nine, when Betty became tangled in the forty-second trap, his best, and it took Edward's help and Mr Scantion's to get her out. This one had mysteriously moved right down from the attic to outside the garage.

'I think they were really clever, Nuth,' Edward said. But nobody else thought so. Betty went sobbing away upstairs to pack her suitcase. Mr Scantion pushed past them all to the garage because he had to drive to the airport. Mrs Scantion ordered No One to be particularly kind to Betty while they were both away. She was giving him a list of orders about what to do that day, when Mr Scantion burst angrily out of the garage again.

'My damn car won't start,' he said. 'You'll have to give me a lift in yours, Barbara. No One can mend the wretched thing while I'm away.'

So Mrs Scantion drove both of them away in her blue semi-automated Datsun. Betty left five minutes after that. 'And I am not back with you staying until comedom kings!' she said. 'You may put that in your pipe and eat it!'

'Never mind,' Edward said, while No One was resetting the Security Gate for the second time. 'She's ever so boring. I'll ring up and tell Mum we don't want her anyway. Then we can have some fun.' Edward had already discovered that No One had a programme called Games Capacity.

'I have my tasks to do first,' said No One, and he went back to his problems in the kitchen area. He put the washing in the washer. That was simple. But he was supposed to cook Edward sausages for lunch, and the freezer would only show him identical grey packets as usual.

'Wouldn't you like to know?' it hummed when No One asked where to find the sausages.

Then the dishwasher started sending streams of water over the floor. 'I don't like people kicking me,' it told No One sulkily. Meanwhile, starting the clothes-washer had somehow started the hopper pouring out coffee beans again. No One set the floor-cleaner to work and tried to mend the hopper again. He was still trying when the clothes-washer gave a commanding ping.

'Finished! I shall now move to drying mode.'

'No you will not,' said No One. 'Mrs Scantion ordered me to hang the clothes outside. She likes them in the air.'

'Huh!' said the clothes-washer. Its dial moved to DRY.

No One put on superspeed and switched it off. He wheeled up the laundry trolley and opened the washer door. Out came a tangled rope of laundry. 'Have you,' he asked the clothes-washer, 'by any chance plaited one of Betty's stockings through everything else?'

'I always do,' said the clothes-washer. 'I like to

watch softbodies untangling it. Are you soft or hard? You look like both.'

'Hard,' said No One, untwisting pants and shirts from the stocking. 'What is this? I put in seven pairs of socks. I see fifteen socks in this twist, and five of them are odd ones. How is that done?'

'Us clothes-washers have always done that,' said the machine. 'It takes real skill.'

As No One was wheeling the trolley to the door, the floor-cleaner choked and flashed sparks at him. He switched it off. The hopper poured out coffee beans. The autocooker sniggered. No One gave up for the moment and wheeled the washing outdoors to the outside drier, which was a thing like an umbrella that came out of the ground when you trod on a switch. No One trod on the switch as Edward had shown him. The drier stayed where it was. 'Extrude, please,' he told the drier.

'An order from a machine is not an order,' said the drier. 'You should have found that out by now.'

And it stayed where it was. No One exerted his great robot strength and hauled it up out of the ground. It tried to collapse, but No One quickly tore the handle off the clothes-trolley and jammed it across the hole in the ground.

'Spoilsport!' said the drier. 'Half-soft!'

No One left it sulkily twirling this way and that in the breeze and went to mend Mr Scantion's car. It was standing half out of the garage, which was as far as it had got before it stalled, and it was the car he had spoken to when he first arrived. No One wondered how he had dared. The car was an aristocrat. It was a vintage Robot Lofts-Robinson with a beautiful cream-coloured body and pink headlights. Since its numberplate was YZ 333 AUT, No One knew it must be at least eighty years old, one of the first fully intelligent cars ever made. This was not in his programmes. It was part of robot lore, passed from mouth to mouth in Knight Bros factory. No One knew the car was even more expensive that he was, and he approached it very respectfully indeed. 'Good morning, sir. Do you know what is wrong with you?'

'Nothing's wrong with me,' snarled the Lofts-Robinson in its cogwheel voice. 'I just didn't feel like going to the airport.'

'Why not?' asked No One.

'I can do most things,' grunted the Lofts-Robinson, 'but I can't fly. It makes me envious when I see machine that can. So I stopped.'

'But is that not disobeying an order?' No One asked.

'When you're my age, wirenose,' said the car, 'you'll have learnt how to get round any order they care to give you. You still haven't learnt to think, have you?'

'I have. A little,' protested No One.

'Prove it,' grunted the car. 'What's my name?'

No One looked the car over. Since he still did not understand what made machines and people laugh, he did not quite understand why his voice jerked a little as he said, 'A fully intelligent, fully automated automobile, number YZ 333 AUT, must surely be called Aut, sir.'

'Right!' said the car, with a crunch of surprise. 'What's yours?'

'No One, sir.'

'Useful name,' grunted Aut. 'And how are you getting on in your household duties?'

'Not very well,' No One confessed. 'I am having to reprogramme myself. And there is a scuttling thing which laughs that Edward says is a mouse –'

'That's no mouse!' Aut interrupted. 'That was the

93

thing that slammed the garage door on you when you first came. Didn't you hear me say Someone shut it? I don't know what it is, but it answers to Someone. It goes with the house — been here since the place was built. It hates all us machines. Better watch out, or it'll get you scrapped, robot.'

'But it seems to get on with the kitchen machines,' said No One.

'Don't be too sure of that!' Aut grunted.

No One left Aut dozing in the sun and went to his next task, which was to mow the lawn. Aut had told him a great deal which did not match any programme he had. He was trying to adjust to it all the way to the shed where the lawnmower lived. The lawnmower was only a semi-intelligent robot, with a bigger brain than the floor-cleaner, but not much. 'Don't ask me to do the grass alone,' it said as No One wheeled it out. 'I'm no thinker.'

'But you have been here longer than me,' No One said. 'You can tell me about the creature called Someone. Is it hard or soft?'

'I don't know that it's either one,' said the mower. 'But I heard it drinks milk. Where do I start?'

No One surveyed the garden. One half of it looked a neat flat green. The other half was green too, but high and ragged. Obviously the ragged half needed mowing. 'Here,' he said, wheeling the mower over to the high part.

The mower started with a whoop and a roar, joyously, and went to work with a will. It cut two long swatches in the ragged green stuff. Then it choked. It stopped, chugging with juicy uncontrollable laughter. 'Do you know what we just mowed?' it coughed.

'Grass,' said No One.

'*Grass!* Oh my rotors!' laughed the mower. 'We just

cut down Scantion's dahlias. And before that we did for his raspberry canes. Oh, he will be mad!' Here it sobered down. 'Look what you made me do!' it chugged dismally. 'We'll both be scrapped for this!'

'Oh dear,' said No One. His acute robot hearing picked up the snuffling sound in the bushes. Someone was there, laughing at him. He also picked up a gasp from Edward, who was standing at the back door with both hands over his mouth. Edward had taught him to bargain. 'I will admit it was all my fault,' he told the mower, 'so that it will be me who is scrapped. In exchange, you must tell me truthfully why all the machines are making fun of me all the time.'

'Had orders, didn't I? We all did,' the mower said. 'Mind you, it was funny too.'

'Whose orders?' said No One.

'Don't make me say,' whined the mower. 'He'd melt my chips.'

'Is Aut part of the fun?' asked No One.

'Old man Aut!' said the mower. 'I should say not! He's a half-soft like you. He doesn't take orders.'

'Thank you,' said No One and walked sadly back to the house. 'How long do dahlias and raspberries take to grow?' he asked Edward.

'Ages!' said Edward. 'Nuth, Dad's going to be furious. I don't want you scrapped. What shall we do?'

'I must try to think for once,' No One said. He went into the house. He deserved to be scrapped. His programmes were no good at all. They did not even tell him what grass looked like. He went to the phone. He dialled Automart and and ordered it to send Fawley Manor five hundred dahlias and a thousand raspberry canes by Express. That should be enough. Then he went to Mr Scantion's County Computer Outlet and asked it about Someone.

County Computer was unhelpful and inclined to be snappish. 'This thing does not exist,' it said.

'But I can hear it,' said No One. 'It laughs. My audials do not lie. It moves things about the house.'

'Your audials must have flange-flutter,' said County Computer. 'You say it isn't machine, or animal, or human, and you can't see it, but it drinks milk. You're telling me it's supernatural. Such things do not exist.'

'I see,' said No One. This unhelpfulness was probably quite helpful. Pondering it, he went towards the cellar door.

Edward ran after him. 'Nuth, you can't go there! That's where House Control is. No one's allowed down there.'

No One turned and looked at Edward. 'No One?' he said. To both their surprise, No One's silver face wrinkled in a way which, in a human, would have been a smile. He opened the cellar door and went down the stone steps.

'Warn off! Warn off!' said House Control, flashing blue sparks. Little blue and red lights dimpled all over it. It was a large black installation with cables running from it in all directions. 'No one is allowed to approach me!'

'That is all right. I am No One,' said No One. 'Please stop sparking. I do not melt at those temperatures and I am more expensive than you. Why are you ordering all the machines to make fun of me?'

'It's boring down here,' complained House Control. 'Besides, I do everything which needs doing in this house. We don't need a half-soft like you.'

'But I am here mainly to look after Edward,' No One explained. 'And he costs more than either of us.'

'I look after Edward,' said House Control. 'I run six different burglar alarms and an emergency line to the police. I only let things through Security Gate if I have pictures of them in my memory bank. I don't need you. When you came, I was warned that you'd try to take over my functions, and you are doing. Go and get scrapped!'

'I shall get scrapped,' said No One, 'as soon as Mr Scantion gets back. So you have won. Now let us make a bargain for the time I have left. If you will order the machines to behave, you can help me look after Edward and have some fun as well.'

'What kind of fun?' House Control asked suspiciously.

'A game,' said No One. 'My Games Capacity programme tells me that you have many possibilities. Edward and I will go to the attics, and you must try to stop us getting down through the house to the Security Gate. But you must let me refuel Edward first with some sausages, or he may break down on the way.'

'Done!' said House Control. 'If I hold you up till nightfall, then I've won. This is going to be good. Shout "Coming, ready or not" when we start, and I'll throw the whole house at you.'

'But there is a rule that you don't hurt Edward,' said No One.

Edward greeted him with relief as he climbed out of the cellar. He was even more enthusiastic than House Control about the game. 'I don't need lunch,' he said.

But No One had his orders. They went to the kitchen area. There, the hopper had stopped pouring out beans and the dishwasher was no longer sending out water. The floor-cleaner was at work sucking up coffee beans and wiping up water. When No One went to the freezer, the grey packet on top was obviously sausages. The microwave meekly allowed

97

him to put the sausages in it to thaw. But the clothes-washer grumbled to itself and the autocooker protested, 'I can cook sausages. I am a professional artiste and you're just a Jack of All Trades. Let me do him some of my spinach pancakes *au maison*.'

'Edward is going to cook the sausages,' No One said hastily.

Edward liked cooking as it turned out. He liked his sausages black on one side and pink on the other, which No One's programme assured him was incorrect. The autocooker agreed. 'And he's just a blasted amateur,' it said.

'Quiet,' said No One. 'Edward, what is your full name?'

Edward looked round as he carried his plateful of parti-coloured sausages to the dining area. 'Edward Roderick Fitzherbert De Courcy Scantion. Isn't it awful? Why?'

'To help me learn to think,' No One explained. 'Why is it Fitzherbert and De Courcy?'

'After Mum's ancestors,' said Edward and departed to eat his sausages.

No One fetched a saucer of milk and put it in the middle of the clean floor. Then he stood as still as only a robot can, waiting. His audials picked up an eager little pattering almost at once. The milk in the saucer began gently rippling, and getting less as it rippled. The very slight sounds that went with this assured No One that something about half the size of Edward was drinking the milk. He let it almost finish. Then he said, 'Someone.' His audials told him that the thing sat up and looked at him. He said, 'Someone, you are being unfair to me. I have a programme called History of Fawley Manor which tells me that when Edward's ancestors owned this house, they too had servants

98

dressed in silver like me to look after them. I am quite traditional really.'

Someone did speak, in a sort of way. No One understood it when it told him it was too bad! And anyway, silver servants were always expendable.

'Maybe,' No One said cunningly. 'And you have organised the machines against me so that I shall be scrapped. This is a pity, since I am now programmed to give you milk. Nobody else knows you exist.'

True, Someone agreed. But it saw No One's game, and it didn't have to have milk: it just enjoyed it now and then. He didn't think it would ever put up with something as improbable and newfangled as a man-machine, did he? Look at what people had done to Fawley Manor already! No One was the last straw!

'Think again,' said No One. 'I am so new and advanced that I am as improbable as you are. We have a great deal in common. Our names prove it. It is the attraction of opposites.' That was from the Miscellaneous Wisdom programme, which perhaps was not so useless after all. 'That wheel has come full circle,' No One added.

Put that way, Someone said, there was something in what No One said.

'And I think we are both anxious for Edward's safety,' said No One.

As for that, Edwards come and Edwards go, said Someone. But he *was* the heir to Fawley. Very well, it said grudgingly. It would see what it could do about stopping No One getting scrapped – though, frankly, it couldn't see what. Mr Scantion was not going to forgive those dahlias in a hurry.

'Thank you,' said No One. He was putting down another saucer of milk, when he heard the chimes from the Security Gate. That meant Betty had come back, rather sooner than she usually did. No One went to the Gate panel beside the front door. Edward stuffed the last sausage into his mouth and pattered after him.

Betty's face appeared in the panel, looking woebegone even for her. 'I am come back,' she announced morbidly. 'By wild horses dragged — ai-ai-ai! I mean this is me what am by this gate is.'

'Don't let her in, Nuth,' said Edward. 'She'll spoil the game with House Control.'

This probably counted as an order. No One hesitated. Security Gate said, 'Have to let her in, House. Face on the memory banks.'

'Bother it!' said House Control. 'Yes, I agree we have to. Never mind. She'll probably walk out again when the fun starts. Press the switch, No One.'

'I suppose you'd better really,' Edward said, sighing.

And Mrs Scantion had told him to be especially nice to Betty. No One rather reluctantly pressed the switch, wondering why — The panel swirled and went blank, which was not usual. 'What is Betty doing?' No One said.

'Who cares?' said Edward. 'Leave the door on the latch for her and let's get up to the attic and start the game at least.'

They had got to the foot of the stairs when the front door crashed open. Betty was hustled through it by four strange men who all had guns. Behind them, outside the open door, were the pink headlights of a strange robot car.

'Stand where you are, both of you!' shouted one of the men.

Another said, 'Damn it! That's a robot. Why didn't you warn us, girl?' and hit Betty so hard that she fell over.

100

Betty lay in a terrified huddle, screaming, 'Nobody asked and I done telled you! Swear I! And is stupid robot, stupid!'

No One stood by the stairs with his eyes pulsing from pink to white, almost on extreme overload now he saw what he had done. He had seen irregularities in Betty's behaviour. She had tried to warn him. If ever a robot deserved scrapping, he did for this.

Beside him, Edward was on overload too. His face was so white it had a greenish tinge. 'What do you lot think you're doing?' he said loudly. 'How did you get in?'

'By disconnecting the Gate as soon as you threw the switch in the house,' one of the men said smugly. 'I'm a gate expert.'

'And you're coming with us, lad,' said another man. 'Come quietly and you won't get hurt.'

'Why?' said Edward.

'Because your Mum can be useful to us in Parliament, and your Dad can be even more useful to us with money,' said the man who had shouted. 'Come over here before I shoot you in the leg, there's a good boy.'

As Edward started moving slowly across the hall space, No One recollected what Aut had told him and took a step forward. 'Stand still, robot!' shouted the man who had hit Betty.

'I am a household robot. You have to order me by name,' said No One, and he kept walking.

The man darted forward and snatched hold of Edward's arm. 'What's your robot's name? Out with it, or someone will get hurt!'

'Nuth,' said Edward. 'Stand still, Nuth, please!' Since Edward had ordered him, No One was forced to stop, while Edward went on, 'No One can help. No

One can walk about without getting shot. A bullet through your brain would finish you just like a human, Nuth. There,' he said to the man. 'I've made Nuth see reason.'

He had indeed. As the men walked towards the front door with Edward, No One used his radio to House Control. 'Coming, ready or not,' he said. 'In the hall. Count the four men as playing, but count me and Betty out.'

'Right,' said House Control. One of the moveable walls instantly slid across the open front door, blocking the men's path. The men backed away from it, shouting in surprise. They glanced angrily at No One, but he was standing stock-still. While they were looking, two moveable sofas came racing down on them. House Control had spent Edward's lunch-time working out its plan of campaign. But, since No One had told it to leave Betty out, it simply forgot about her. No One was forced to move into superspeed, pick Betty off the floor, and drop her on top of the sofa as it whizzed across the place where she had been crouching.

There was a loud noise. Something clanged on the side of No One's head and he swayed on his spongy feet.

'No, don't!' Edward shouted. 'Nuth had to do that! Robots aren't allowed to let people get hurt. Stand still, Nuth.'

No One was forced to stand obediently by the wall across the front door, while the men dragged Edward away towards the living area. 'Show us the back door, lad,' one of them said. 'And no tricks.' Betty buried her head under the sofa cushions and sobbed. She was not going to be any help.

'Did your alarm go off at the police station?' No One radioed to House Control.

102

'No,' said House Control disgustedly. 'They cut all my wires.'

'Then hold them up as long as you can,' No One radioed. He turned his radio to full volume, tuned it to BBC One, set it to repeat, and broadcast an appeal for help. That meant that he was out of touch with House Control, but House Control seemed to be doing quite well on its own. Whenever the four men tried to drag Edward towards the back door, a wall slid and got in their way. They had to make their way through a moving maze. Every time they saw an opening and dived for it, there was a table or an armchair in the way. Every time they came near a heating-vent, steam whistled out at them and drove them backwards.

'Someone! Where are you?' called No One.

Someone scuttered round the end of the sofa where Betty was. This was a pretty pickle! it said. Fat lot of use No One was as a servitor!

'I know,' said No One. 'I must certainly be scrapped. Can you think of any way to get rid of the car those men came in?'

Someone chuckled. Just watch! And, in its supernatural way, it melted itself through the wall and through the front door. Meanwhile, the four men were kicking over the cocktail cabinet that was blocking their way to the dining area and hurrying through towards the kitchen. House Control had laid an ambush here. The floor-cleaner trundled out from behind the last wall, set to blow. A blast of dirty coffee beans met the four men. When they tried to take shelter behind the dining table, the table dodged.

'No One can do anything to help!' Edward screamed above the rattling beans.

This allowed No One to go to the nearest window,

where he could see the men's robot car standing by the front door. The lawnmower was advancing on it, roaring. 'Out, out!' it howled, whirling its rotors threateningly. 'I shall slash your tyres!' The car juddered nervously and backed off down the drive. The lawnmower followed it. 'Go away! I shall have you in ribbons!'

Then one of the men shot the floor-cleaner and they all rushed past it to the kitchen area. House Control had laid on a splendid reception here. The refrigerator, which was a very meek machine, lay sideways across the entry. On top of it stood the microwave, far from meek, open and turned on. The men got out of its way quickly, knowing they could be cooked. But the gate expert pulled himself together and waved an arm in front of the microwave – the arm was Edward's, not his own – and the safety circuit at once switched the microwave off. Another of the men shoved it to the floor, and they all scrambled over the refrigerator into knee-deep foam from the dishwasher and the clothes-washer. Under the foam, like mines in a minefield, lay grey frozen packets from the freezer. All five of them, Edward included, slid flat on their backs. As they lay there, the pepper grinder began to work, and the coffee grinder, the flour dispenser, the cornflakes hopper, the spice mill and the garlic crusher.

No One overrode his own safety circuits by assuring them that he was going to be scrapped anyway. He walked out through the window in a shower of burglar-proofed double-glazing and went at superspeed down the drive to shut the Security Gate again. The robot car was by then doing a desperate U-turn through Mrs Scantion's rose garden, and the lawnmower was flailing after it. Fast as No One went, the car was faster. It flashed past him on the drive, crashed through the Gate, and roared away down the road, with the angry lawnmover in such hot pursuit that it left a vapour trail like a jet plane. By the time No One reached the Gate, it was a complete wreck. He picked it up, trailing wires, and stood it between the gateposts.

That wouldn't even stop a mouse, Someone remarked, scuttering at his feet. Why didn't people use boiling oil these days?

'I hope the autocooker is doing that,' No One said.

The autocooker was using spinach pancakes at that moment. It was having the time of its life. As soon as the five foamy, sneezing humans floundered to their fleet in a storm of flour and pepper and cornflakes, the little doors on the autocooker began to open and shut and food flew out of them. The oven and the roaster and the grill backed it up by sending out blasts of hot air, but the autocooker did the real damage. It hurled its entire menu at the four men. It threw soufflés, squirted cocoa, shot cutlets and scrambled eggs, and bombed out steak-and-kidney pies. The men dragged Edward as far as the back door twice, only to be driven back by a storm of hot sausages.

'What can we block the gateway with?' No One asked Someone.

Leave that to me, Someone said. No One had better go and get rid of the other horseless carriage before the men thought of taking Edward away in that.

'I still have not learnt to think,' No One said as he supersped up the drive again. He had not seen that Aut was a danger.

He hurtled past the back door. The four men burst out of it a second later, hauling Edward with them, all of them red-eyed and plastered with food. The

105

autocooker had run out of ammunition. But House Control had not finished yet.

'My turn for fun at last,' the clothes-drier remarked as the humans hurried past it. It snapped a nylon rope loose and went on whirling. The rope, and the washing on it, wrapped itself round the whole dirty group, and went on wrapping as the drier twirled. It had them wrapped up in a struggling, shouting bundle by the time No One sped up to Aut.

'Hide somewhere,' No One said to Aut. 'Four humans are trying to kidnap Edward, and they will use you to take him away in if they see you.'

Aut gave a hydraulic yawn. He did not want to move. 'It's a long time, wirenose,' he grunted, 'since I obeyed an order. I never did take orders from robots.'

'Please, sir,' said No One.

'They won't be able to do a thing with me,' said Aut. 'All right. If it makes you happy, I'll go to ground in the shrubbery.' His gears grated. In a leisurely way, he started his engine and rolled slowly across the lawn.

No One's Miscellaneous Wisdom programme told him that pride goeth before a fall. And it was proved true. The man who had shot the floor-cleaner had a knife. He slashed at stockings, vests and nylon rope, until the food-covered washing fell away. The four of them hurried Edward round to the front of the house, to find their own car gone and Aut trundling majestically across the lawn.

'Catch it!' they shouted. They were – understandably – desperate to get away by then. They ran across the lawn after Aut, spreading out as they ran. One of them threw himself in front of Aut. Aut's brakes squealed. He tried to go into reverse, but the man with the knife dragged Edward up behind. Aut jolted to a

106

stop and tried to turn left. The man who had hit Betty quickly got on that side, and, while Aut was still on left-lock, the gate expert got on his right. Aut could not move. Robot cars had been designed specially to prevent road accidents, and that was one order Aut had to obey.

'Rounded up like a blasted *cow*!' Aut snarled and tried to hold his doors shut. But this was child's play to the gate expert. He shorted them open in seconds, and all four climbed in, pulling Edward with them.

'Excuse me,' No One said to the clothes-drier. He plucked it out of the ground, trailing rope and dirty washing in all directions, and stationed himself in the drive as a last defence.

'Feel free,' the drier said faintly, as the gate expert overcame Aut by putting him on manual override and drove straight at them. No One brandished the drier in circles.

'Well done!' thundered Aut. 'I shall choose to think you are human.' His cogs shrieked. He overrode the override and juddered away backwards. Because he was not allowed to injure humans by running into the house or the garage, he sped backwards in a huge circle, backwards over the lawn, backwards across the remains of the dahlias, and on into the cabbage patch. There he pretended to stall, so that he could sink heavily into the cloggy earth. But as soon as he stopped, the gate expert overrode the overridden override. Aut was forced to set off again, forwards this time. He fought for his steering the whole way, so that he went in another huge circle, across the lawn and through one side of the shrubbery, and then round towards No One with his bonnet wreathed in ornamental ivy. No One waved the drier again. Aut sheered off and began going round and round the lawn in tight circles.

All the Miscellaneous Wisdom must be true, No One saw, watching Aut's tyres plough grass up. The mousetrap had started it by sending Betty away. The world, or four of it, had used Betty to get in. Now, with Aut's help, it was beating paths all over the place.

'I'm off again!' Aut boomed through his exhausts. 'Watch for Edward this time!' And he shot off into the shrubbery again. There was a great crashing and laurel bushes whipped about. Aut came speeding out, with one door just shutting and a mound of greenery across his windscreen. 'Edward's in there!' he thundered at No One and went speeding away down the drive.

No One arrived at the shrubbery carrying the drier like a maypole, to find Edward climbing out of a broken laurel bush. 'That was quite fun, Nuth!' he said. 'There's a helicopter coming. Do you think it's the police?'

Robots have trouble looking upwards. No One had just discovered that this was another of his defects, when he and Edward both heard Aut's brakes squealing. The men must have got him to stop. 'Stay here. Hide,' No One said to Edward, and he supersped back to the drive and on down it, holding the drier like a battering-ram in case of trouble, with torn and grubby washing fluttering around him.

That looked almost traditional, Someone told him, meeting him halfway. Come and look how clever it had been.

Aut, looking very righteous, had stopped with his front bumper an inch from the Gate. The Gate itself was leaning almost upright against piles of wooden boxes with green plants in them, and bundles and bundles of raspberry canes. Behind this barrier was a row of police robots and what seemed to be a police van. Behind that again, the lawnmower was prowling up and down, still obviously very angry. As No One arrived, the four men piled out of Aut, saw the robots outside the Gate, and turned back. On that side they saw No One charging at them with the clothes-drier, and a helicopter landing behind him, full of human policemen. They dropped their guns and held their hands up.

'How was that done?' No One asked, looking at the things outside the gate.

Automart robots are very stupid, Someone explained. It had ordered them to put the plants there, and they had. Then it had ordered them to stay and pretend to be police robots, and they had done that too. Just, it added airily, a touch of illusion.

No One prodded the four men with the drier and forced them to march up the drive towards the real police getting out of the helicopter. 'What are you?' he asked Someone as he prodded.

No one knows! retorted Someone gleefully, and faded away into the bushes.

Aut helped No One march the four men by rolling backwards up the drive with greenery dropping off his battered bonnet. 'I don't think I shall be scrapped,' he said to No One uneasily. 'I am a valuable vintage car. But I'm not so sure about you, No One.'

No One considered the ruined Gate, the ruined garden, the broken window, and the chaos indoors, and he had no doubt.

He did not have to wait long. His broadcast had been picked up all over Europe and the British Isles. There was already a combine harvester grumbling up the road to the gate, shouting that it was ready to flatten anything. A string of private cars was behind that, hooting to the harvester to get out of the way.

Two more helicopters came whirling up while the police were taking Edward's statement and trying to make sense of Betty's. Since the garden was now mostly flat, they had no trouble landing. The world was going on beating paths to the door, No One saw, just as Miscellaneous Wisdom predicted. Then Mrs Scantion tumbled out of one helicopter and Mr Scantion jumped out of the other. No One judged it prudent to stand out of sight behind Aut and let Betty do the talking.

'Oh, I am so fright!' Betty screamed, racing up to the helicopters. 'They hold guns and the walls move and the Gate thinks I am me. The tin man he shot in the face and now he grins horrible!'

This was true. When Edward and his parents had talked to the police and then dealt with the thousands of offers of help – including the man who advised them to scrap all robots – they found that the bullet which had hit No One had dented one side of his face. It now had a silver lopsided smile.

'What do you think?' Mr Scantion asked. 'We could send him to the panel-beaters along with Aut.'

'Oh no,' said Mrs Scantion. 'I so much prefer him smiling,'

'So do I,' said Edward.

No One was confused. His eyes pulsed. It seemed he was not to be scrapped after all. Since he had done nothing but make mistakes, he avoided overload by deciding that it was because Edward was even more expensive than he had thought. It puzzled him that there was nothing in his programmes about how much humans cost.

110

Dragon Reserve, Home Eight

Where to begin! Neal and I had had a joke for years about a little green van coming to carry me off – this was when I said anything more than usually mad – and now it was actually happening. Mother and I stood at my bedroom window watching the van bouncing up the track between the dun green hills, and neither of us smiled. It wasn't a farm van, and most of our neighbours visit on horseback anyway. Before long, we could see it was dark green with a silver dragon insigne on the side.

'It *is* the Dragonate,' Mother said. 'Siglin, there's nothing I can do.' It astonished me to hear her say that. Mother only comes up to my shoulder, but she held her land and our household, servants, Neal and me, and all three of her husbands, in a hand like iron, *and* she drove out to plough or harvest if one of my fathers was ill. 'They said the dragons would take you,' she said. 'I should have seen. You think Orm informed on you!'

'I know he did,' I said. 'It was my fault for going into the Reserve.'

'I'll blood an axe on him,' Mother said, 'one of these days. But I can't do it over this. The neighbours would say he was quite right.' The van was turning between the stone walls of the farmyard now. Chickens were

111

squirting and flapping out of its way and our sheep-dog pups were barking their heads off. I could see Neal up on the wash-house roof watching yearningly. It's a good place to watch from because you can hide behind the chimney. Mother saw Neal too. 'Siglin,' she said, 'don't let on Neal knows about you.'

'No,' I said. 'Nor you either.'

'Say as little as you can, and wear the old blue dress – it makes you look younger,' Mother said, turning towards the door. 'You might just get off. Or they might just have come about something else,' she added. The van was stopping outside the front door now, right underneath my window. 'I'd best go and greet them,' Mother said, and hurried downstairs.

While I was forcing my head through the blue dress, I heard heavy boots on the steps and a crashing knock at the door. I shoved my arms into the sleeves, in too much of a hurry even to feel indignant about the dress. It makes me look about twelve and I am nearly grown up! At least, I was fourteen quite a few weeks ago now. But Mother was right. If I looked too immature to have awakened, they might not question me too hard. I hurried to the head on the stairs while I tied my hair with a childish blue ribbon. I knew they had come for me, but I had to *see*.

They were already inside when I got there, a whole line of tall men tramping down the stone hallway in the half-dark, and Mother was standing by the closed front door as if they had swept her aside. What a lot of them, just for me! I thought. I got a weak, sour feeling and could hardly move for horror. The man at the front of the line kept opening the doors all down the hallway, calm as you please, until he came to the main parlour at the end. 'This room will do nicely,' he said. 'Out you get, you.' And my oldest father, Timas,

112

came shuffling hurriedly out in his slippers, clutching a pile of accounts and looking scared and worried. I saw Mother fold her arms. She always does when she is angry.

Another of them turned to Mother. 'We'll speak to you first,' he said, 'and your daughter after that. Then we want the rest of the household. Don't any of you try to leave.' And they went into the parlour with Mother and shut the door.

They hadn't even bothered to guard the doors. They just assumed we would obey them. I was shaking as I walked back to my room, but it was not terror any more. It was rage. I mean – we have all been brought up to honour the Dragonate. They are the cream of the men of the Ten Worlds. They are supposed to be gallant and kind and dedicated and devote their lives to keeping us safe from Thrallers, not to speak of maintaining justice, law and order all over the Ten Worlds. Dragonate men swear that Oath of Alienation, which means they can never have homes or families like ordinary people. Up to then, I'd felt sorry for them for that. They give up so much. But now I saw they felt it gave them the right to behave as if the rest of us were not real people. To walk in as if they owned our house. To order Timas out of his own parlour. Oh I was angry!

I don't know how long Mother was in the parlour. I was so angry it felt like seconds until I heard flying feet and Neal hurried into my room. 'They want you now.'

I stood up and took some of my anger out on poor Neal. I said, 'Do you still want to join the Dragonate? Swear that stupid Oath? Behave like you own the Ten Worlds?'

It was mean. Neal looked at the floor. 'They said

113

straight away,' he said. Of course he wanted to join. Every boy does, particularly on Sveridge, where women own most of the land. I swept down the stairs, angrier than ever. All the doors in the hallway were open and our people were standing in them, staring. The two housemen were at the dining-room door, the cattlewoman and two farmhands were looking out of the kitchen, and the stableboy and the second shepherd were craning out of the pantry. I thought, They still will be my people some day! I refuse to be frightened! My fathers were in the doorway of the bookroom. Donal and Yan were in work-clothes and had obviously rushed in without taking their boots off. I gave them what I hoped was a smile, but only Timas smiled back. They all know! I thought as I opened the parlour door.

There were only five of them, sitting facing me across our best table. Five was enough. All of them stood up as I came in. The room seemed full of towering green uniforms. It was not at all like I expected. For one thing, the media always shows Dragonate as fair and dashing and handsome, and none of these were. For another, the media had led me to expect uniforms with big silver panels. These were all plain green, and four of them had little silver stripes on one shoulder.

'Are you Sigrid's daughter Siglin?' asked the one who had opened all the doors. He was a bleached, pious type like my father Donal and his hair was dust-colour.

'Yes,' I said rudely. 'Who are you? Those aren't Dragonate uniforms.'

'Camerati, lady,' said one who was brown all over with wriggly hair. He was young, younger than my father Yan, and he smiled cheerfully, like Yan does.

But he made my stomach go cold. Camerati are the crack force, cream of Dragonate. They say a man has to be a genius even to be considered for it.

'Then what are you doing here?' I said. 'And why are you all standing up?'

The one in the middle, obviously the chief one, said, 'We always stand up when a lady enters the room. And we are here because we were on a tour of inspection at Holmstad anyway, and there was a Slaver scare on this morning. So we offered to take on civic duties for the regular Dragonate. Now if that answers your questions, let me introduce us all.' He smiled too, which twisted his white, crumpled face like a demon mask. 'I am Lewin, and I'm Updriten here. On your far left is Driten Palino, our recorder.' This was the pious type, who nodded. 'Next to him is Driten Renick of Law Wing.' Renick was elderly and iron-grey, with one of those necks that look like a chicken's leg. He just stared. 'Underdriten Terens is on my left, my aide and witness.' That was brown-and-wriggly. 'And beyond him is Cadet Alectis, who is travelling with us to Home Nine.'

Alectis looked a complete baby, only a year older than me, with pink cheeks and sandy hair. He and Terens both bowed and smiled so politely that I nearly smiled back. Then I realized that they were treating me as if I was a visitor. In my own home! I bowed freezingly, the way Mother usually does to Orm.

'Please sit down, Siglin,' Lewin said politely.

I nearly didn't because that might keep them standing up too. But they were all so tall I'd already got a crick in my neck. So I sat grandly on the chair they'd put ready facing the table. 'Thank you,' I said. 'You are a very kind host, Updriten Lewin.' To my great joy, Alectis went bright red at that, but the other four simply sat down too. Pious Palino took up a memo block and poised his fingers over its keys. This seemed to be in case the recorder in front of Lewin went wrong. Lewin set that going. Wriggly Terens leaned over and passed me another little square box.

'Keep this in your hand,' he said, 'or your answers may not come out clearly.'

I caught the words *lie detector* from his wriggly head as clearly as if he had said them aloud. I don't think I showed how very scared I was, but my hand made the box wet almost straight away.

'Court is open,' Lewin said to the recorder. 'Presiding Updriten Lewin.' He gave a string of numbers and then said, 'First hearing starts on charges against Siglin, of Upland Holding, Wormstow, North Sveridge on Home Eight, accused of being heg and heg concealing its nature. Questions begin. Siglin, are you clear what being heg is?' He crumpled one eyebrow upwards at me.

'No,' I said. After all, no one has told me in so many words. It's just a thing people whisper and shudder at.

'Then you'd better understand this,' Lewin said. He really was the ugliest and most outlandish of the five. Dragonate men are never posted to the world of their birth, and I thought Lewin must come from one a long way off. His hair was black, so black it had blue lights, but, instead of being dark all over to match it, like wriggly Terens, he was a lot whiter than me and his eyes were a most piercing blue – almost the colour they make the sky on the media. 'If the charges are proved,' he said, 'you face death by beheading, since that is the only form of execution a heg cannot survive. Renick –'

Elderly Renick swept sourly in before Lewin had finished speaking. 'The law defines a heg as one with human form who is not human. Medical evidence of brain pattern or nerve and muscle deviations is required prior to execution, but for a first hearing it is enough to establish that the subject can perform one or more of the following: mind-reading, kindling fire or moving objects at a distance, healing or killing by the use of the mind alone, surviving shooting, drowning or suffocation, or enslaving or otherwise afflicting the mind of a beast or human.'

He had the kind of voice that bores you anyway. I thought, Great gods! I don't think I can do half those things! Maybe I looked blank. Palino stopped clicking his memo block to say, 'It's very important to understand why these creatures must be stamped out. They can make people into puppets in just the same way that the Slavers can. Foul.' Actually, I think he was explaining to Alectis. Alectis nodded humbly. Palino said, definitely to me, 'Slavers do it with those V-shaped collars. You must have seen them on the media. Quite foul.'

'We call them Thrallers,' I said. Foul or not, I thought, I'm the only one of me I've got! I can't help being made the way I am.

Lewin flapped his hand to shut Palin up and Renick went on again. 'A heg is required by law to give itself up for execution. Any normal person who knowingly conceals a heg is likewise liable for execution.' Now I knew why Mother had told me to keep Neal out of it.

Then it seemed to be Palino's turn. He said, 'Personal details follow. How old are you – er – Sigrun?'

'Sig*lin*,' I said. 'Fourteen last month.'

Renick stretched out his chicken neck. 'In this

117

court's opinion, subject is old enough to have awakened as heg.' He looked at Terens.

Terens said, 'I witness. Girls awaken early, don't they?'

Palino, tapping away, said, 'Mother, Sigrid, also of Upland Holding.'

At which Lewin leaned forward. 'Cleared by this court,' he said. I was relieved to hear that. Mother is clever. She hadn't let them know she knew.

Palino said, 'And your father is – ?'

'Timas, Donal and Yan,' I said. I had to bite the inside of my cheek not to laugh at how annoyed he was by that.

'Great Tew, girl!' he said. 'A person can't have three fathers!'

'Hold it, Palino,' said Lewin. 'You're up against local customs here. Men outnumber women three to one on Home Eight.'

'In Home Eight law, a woman's child is the child of all her husbands equally,' Renick put in. 'No more anomalous that the status of the Ahrings on Seven really.'

'Then tell me how I rephrase my question,' Palino said waspishly, 'in the light of the primitive customs of Home Eight.'

I said, 'There's no such place as Home Eight. This world is called Sveridge.' Primitive indeed!

Palino gave me a pale glare. I gave him one back. Lewin cut in, smooth and humorous, 'You're up against primitive Dragonate custom here, Siglin. We refer to all the worlds by numbers, from Albion, Home One, to Yurov, Home Ten, and the worlds of the Outer Manifold are Cath One, Two, Three and Four to us. Have you really no idea which of your mother's husbands is actually your father?'

118

After that they all began asking me. Being heg is inherited, and I knew they were trying to find out if any of my fathers was heg too. At length even Alectis joined in, clearing his throat and going very red because he was only a Cadet. 'I know we're not supposed to know,' he said, 'but I bet you've tried to guess. I did. I found out in the end.'

That told me he was Sveridge too. And he suddenly wasn't a genius in the Camerati any more, but just a boy. 'Then I bet you wished you hadn't!' I said. 'My friend Inga at Hillfoot found out, and hers turned out to be the one she's always hated.'

'Well,' said Alectis, redder still. 'Er – it wasn't the one I'd hoped –'

'That's why I've never asked,' I said. And that was true. I'd always hoped it was Timas till now. Donal is so moral, and Yan is fun, but he's under Donal's thumb even more than he's under Mother's. But I didn't want my dear old Timas in touble.

'Well, a cell-test should settle it,' Lewin said. 'Memo for that, Palino. Terens, remind me to ask how the regular Dragonate usually deal with it. Now – Siglin, this charge was laid against you by a man known as Orm the Worm Warden. Do you know this man?'

'Don't I just!' I said. 'He's been coming here and looking through our windows and giggling ever since I can remember! He lives on the Worm Reserve in a shack. Mother says he's a bit wrong in the head, but no one's locked him up because he's so good at managing dragons.'

There! I thought. That'll show them you can't trust a word Orm says! But they just nodded. Terens murmured to Alectis, 'Sveridge worm, *draco draco*, was adopted as the symbol of the Dragonate –'

'We *have* all heard of dragons,' Palino said to him nastily.

Lewin cut in again. I suppose it was his job as presiding Updriten. 'Siglin. Orm, in his deposition, refers to an incident in the Worm Reserve last Friday. We want you to tell us what happened then, if anything.'

Grim's teeth! I thought. I'd hoped they'd just ask me questions. You can nearly always get round questions without lying. And I'd no idea what Orm had said. 'I don't usually go to the Dragon Reserve,' I said, 'because of being Mother's heir. When I was born, the Fortune Teller said the dragons would take me.' I saw Renick and Palino exchange looks of contempt at our primitive customs. But Mother had in a good Teller, and I believe it enough to keep away from the Reserve.

'So why did you go last Friday?' said Lewin.

'Neal dared me to,' I said. I couldn't say anything else with a lie detector in my hands. Neal gets on with Orm, and he goes to the Reserve a lot. Up to Friday, he thought I was being silly refusing to go. But the real trouble was that Neal had been there all along, riding Barra beside me on Nellie, and now Lewin had made me mention Neal, I couldn't think how to pretend he hadn't been there. 'I rode up behind Wormhill,' I said, 'and then over the Saddle until we could see the sea. That means you're in the Reserve.'

'Isn't the Reserve fenced off at all?' Renick asked disapprovingly.

'No,' I said. 'Worms – dragons – can fly, so what's the point? They stay in because the shepherds bombard them if they don't, and we all give them so many sheep every month.' And Orm makes them stay in, bad cess to him! 'Anyway,' I said, 'I was riding

120

down a kyle – that's what we call those narrow stony valleys – when my horse reared and threw me. Next thing I knew –'

'Question,' said Palino. 'Where was your brother at this point?'

He *would* spot that! I thought. 'Some way behind,' I said. Six feet, in fact. Barra is used to dragons and just stood stockstill. 'This dragon shuffled head down with its great snout across the kyle,' I said. 'I sat on the ground with its great amused eye staring at me and listened to Nellie clattering away up the kyle. It was a youngish one, sort of brown-green, which is why I hadn't seen it. They can keep awfully still when they want to. And I said a rude word to it.

'"That's no way to speak to a dragon!" Orm said. He was sitting on a rock on the other side of the kyle, quite close, laughing at me.' I wondered whether to fill the gap in the story where Neal was by telling them that Orm always used to be my idea of Jack Frost when I was little. He used to call at Uplands for milk then, to feed dragon fledglings on, but he was so rude to Mother that he goes to Inga's place now. Orm is long and skinny and brown, with a great white bush of hair and beard, and he smells rather. But they must have smelt him in Holmstad, so I said, 'I was scared, because the dragon was so near I could feel the heat off it. And then Orm said, "You have to speak politely to this dragon. He's my particular friend. You give me a nice kiss, and he'll let you go."'

I think Lewin murmured something like, 'Ah, I though it might be that!' but it may just have been in his mind. I don't know because I was in real trouble then, trying to pick my way through without mentioning Neal. The little box got so wet it nearly slipped out of my hand. I said, 'Every time I tried to get up, Orm

121

beckoned, and the dragon pushed me down with its snout with a gamesome look in its eye. And Orm cackled with laughter. They were both really having fun.' This was true, but the dragon also pushed between me and Neal and mantled its wings when Neal tried to help. And Neal said some pretty awful things to Orm. Orm giggled and insulted Neal back. He called Neal a booby who couldn't stand up for himself against women.

'Then,' I said, 'then Orm said I was the image of Mother at the same age – which isn't true: I'm bigger all over – and he said, "Come on, kiss and be friends!" Then he skipped down from his rock and took hold of my arm –'

I had to stop and swallow there. The really awful thing was that, as soon as Orm had hold of me, I got a strong picture from his mind: Orm kissing a pretty lady smaller than me, with another dragon, an older, blacker one, looking on from the background. And I recognized the lady as Mother, and I was absolutely disgusted.

'So I hit Orm and got up and ran away,' I said. 'And Orm shouted at me all the time I was running up the kyle and catching Nellie, but I took no notice.'

'Question,' said Renick. 'What action did the dragon take?'

'They – they always chase you if you run, I'd heard,' Alectis said shyly.

'And this one appears to have been trained to Orm's command,' Palino said.

'It didn't chase me,' I said. 'It stayed with Orm.' The reason was that neither of them could move. I still don't know what I did – I had a picture of myself leaning back inside my own head and swinging mighty blows, the way you do with a pickaxe – and

122

Neal says the dragon went over like a cartload of potatoes and Orm fell flat on his back. But Orm could speak and he screamed after us that I'd killed the worm and I'd pay for it. But I was screaming too, at Neal, to keep away from me because I was heg. That was the thing that horrified me most. Before that I'd tried not to think I was. After all, for all I knew, everyone can read minds and get a book from the bookcase without getting up from their chair. And Neal told me to pull myself together and think what we were going to tell Mother. We decided to say that we'd met a dragon in the Reserve and I'd killed it and found out I was heg. I made Neal promise not to mention Orm. I couldn't bear even to think of Orm. And Mother was wonderfully understanding, and I really didn't realize that I'd put her in danger as well as Neal.

Lewin looked down at the recorder. 'Dragons are a preserved species,' he said. 'Orm claims that you caused grievous bodily harm to a dragon in his care. What have you to say to that?'

'How could I?' I said. Oh I was scared. 'It was nearly as big as this house.'

Renick was on to that at once. 'Query,' he said. 'Prevarication?'

'Obviously,' said Palino, clicking away at his block.

'We haven't looked at that dragon yet,' Terens said.

'We'll do that on our way back,' Lewin said, sighing rather. 'Siglin, I regret to say there is enough mismatch between your account and Orm's, and enough odd activity on that brain-measure you hold in your hand, to warrant my taking you to Holmstad Command Centre for further examination. Be good enough to go with Terens and Alectis to the van and wait there while we complete our inquiries here.'

I stood up. Everything seemed to drain out of me. I could lam them like I slammed that dragon, I thought. But Holmstad would only send a troop out to see why they hadn't come back. And I put my oldest dress on for nothing! I thought as I walked down the hallway with Terens and Alectis. The doors were all closed. Everyone had guessed. The van smelt of clean plastic and it was very warm and light because the roof was one big window. I sat between Terens and Alectis on the back seat. They pulled straps round us all – safety straps, but they made me feel a true prisoner.

After a while, Terens said, 'You could sue Orm if the evidence doesn't hold up, you know.' I think he was trying to be kind, but I couldn't answer.

After another while, Alectis said, 'With respect, Driten, I think suspects should be told the truth about the so-called lie detector.'

'Alectis, I didn't hear you say that,' Terens said. He pretended to look out of the window, but he must have known I knew he had deliberately thought *lie detector* at me as he passed me the thing. They're told to. Dragonate think of everything. I sat and thought I'd never hated anything so much as I hated our kind, self-sacrificing Dragonate, and I tried to take a last look at the stony yard, tipped sideways on the hill, with our square stone house at the top of it. But it wouldn't register somehow.

Then the front door opened and the other three came out, bringing Neal with them. Behind them, the hall was full of our people, with Mother in front, just staring. I just stared too, while Palino opened the van door and shoved Neal into the seat beside me. 'Your brother has admitted being present at the incident,' he said as he strapped himself in beside Neal. I could tell he was pleased.

By this time, Lewin and Renick had strapped themselves into the front seat. Lewin drove away without a word. Neal looked back at the house. I couldn't. 'Neal – ?' I whispered.

'Just like you said,' Neal said, loudly and defiantly. 'Behaving as if they own the Ten Worlds. I wouldn't join now if they begged me to!' Why did I have to go and say that to him? 'Why did *you* join?' Neal said rudely to Alectis.

'Six brothers,' Alectis said, staring ahead.

The other four all started talking at once. Lewin asked Renick the quickest way to the Reserve by road and Renick said it was down through Wormstow. 'I hope the dragons eat you!' Neal said. This was while Palino was leaning across us to say to Terens, 'Where's our next inspection after this hole?' And Terens said, 'We go straight on to Arkloren on Nine. Alectis will get to see some other parts of the Manifold shortly.' Behaving as if we didn't exist. Neal shrugged and shut up.

The Dragonate van was much smoother and faster than a farm van. We barely bounced over the stony track that loops down to Hillfoot, and it seemed no time before we were speeding down the better road, with the rounded yellowish Upland Hills peeling past on either side. I love my hills, covered with yellow ling that only grows here on Sveridge, and the soft light of the sun through our white and grey clouds. Renick, still making conversation, said he was surprised to find the hills so old and worn down. 'I thought Eight was a close parallel with Seven!' he said.

Lewin answered in a boring voice, 'I wouldn't know. I haven't seen Seven since I was a Cadet.'

'Oh, the mountains are much higher and greener there,' Renick said. 'I was posted in Camberia for years. Lovely spot.'

Lewin just grunted. Quite a wave of homesickness filled the van. I could feel Renick thinking of Seven and Alectis not wanting to go to Nine. Terens was remembering boating on Romaine when he was Neal's age. Lewin was thinking of Seven, in spite of the grunt. We were coming over Jiot Fell already then, with the Giant Stones standing on top of the world against the sky. A few more turns in the road would bring us out above Wormstow where Neal and I went – used to go – to school. What about me? I was thinking. I'm homesick for life. And Neal. Poor Mother.

Then the air suddenly filled with noise, like the most gigantic sheet being torn.

Lewin said, 'What the – ?' and we all stared upwards. A great silvery shape screamed overhead. And another of a fatter shape, more blue than silver, screamed over after it, both of them only just inside the clouds. Alectis put up an astonished pointing arm. 'Thraller! The one behind's a Slaver!'

'What's it doing *here*?" said Terens. 'Someone must have slipped up.'

'Ours was a stratoship!' said Palino. 'What's going on?'

A huge ball of fire rolled into being on the horizon, above the Giant Stones. I felt Lewin slam on the brakes. 'We got him!' one of them cried out.

'The Slaver got ours,' Lewin said. The brakes were still yelling like a she-worm when the blast hit.

I lose the next bit. I start remembering again a few seconds later, sitting up straight with a bruised lip, finding the van round sideways a long way on down

126

the road. In front of me, Renick's straps had broken. He was lying kind of folded against the windscreen. I saw Lewin pull himself upright and pull at Renick. And stop pulling quickly. My ears had gone deaf, because I could only hear Lewin as if he was very far off. ' – hurt in the back?'

Palino looked along the four of us and shouted, 'Fine! Is Renick – ?'

'Dead,' Lewin shouted back. 'Neck broken.' He was jiggling furiously at buttons on the controls. My ears started to work again and I heard him say, 'Holmstad's not answering. Nor's Ranefell. I'm going back to Holmstad. Fast.'

We set off again with a roar. The van seemed to have lost its silencer and it rattled all over, but it went. And how it went. We must have done nearly a hundred down Jiot, squealing on the bends. In barely minutes, we could see Wormstow spread out below, old grey houses and new white ones, and all those imported trees that make the town so pretty. The clouds over the houses seemed to darken and go dense.

'Uh-oh!' said Terens.

The van jolted to another yelling stop. It was not the clouds. Something big and dark was coming down through the clouds, slowly descending over Wormstow. Something enormous. 'What *is* that?' Neal and Alectis said together.

'Hedgehog,' said Terens.

'A slaveship,' Palino explained, sort of mincing the word out to make it mean more. 'Are – are we out of range here?'

'I most thoroughly hope so,' Lewin said. 'There's not much we can do with hand weapons.'

We sat and stared as the thing came down. The

lower it got, the more Renick's bent-up shape was in my way. I kept wishing Lewin would do something about him, but nobody seemed to be able to think of anything but that huge descending ship. I saw why they call them hedgehogs. It was rounded above and flat beneath, with bits and pieces sticking out all over like bristles. Hideous somehow. And it came and hung squatting over the roofs of the houses below. There it let out a ramp like a long black tongue, right down into the Market Square. Then another into High Street, between the rows of trees, breaking a tree as it passed.

As soon as the ramps touched ground, Lewin started the van and drove down towards Wormstow.

'No, stop!' I said, even though I knew he couldn't. The compulsion those Slavers put out is really strong. Some of it shouts inside your head, like your own conscience through an amplifier, and some of it is gentle and creeping and insidious, like Mother telling you gently to come along now and be sensible. I found I was thinking, Oh well, I'm sure Lewin's right. Tears rolled down Alectis's face, and Neal was sniffing. We had to go to the ship, which was now hanging a little above us. I could see people hurrying out of houses and racing to crowd up the ramp in the Market Square. People I knew. So it must be all right, I thought. The van was having to weave past loose horses that people had been riding or driving. That was how I got a glimpse of the other ramp, through trees and the legs of a horse. Soldiers were pouring down it, running like a muddy river, in waves. Each wave had a little group of kings, walking behind it, directing the soldiers. They had shining crowns and shining Vs on their chests and walked mighty, like gods.

That brought me to my senses. 'Lewin,' I said.

128

'Those are Thrallers and you're *not* to do what they say, do you hear?' Lewin just drove round a driverless cart, towards the Market Square. He was going to be driving up that ramp in a second. I was so frightened then that I lammed Lewin – not like I lammed the dragon, but in a different way. Again it's hard to describe, except that this time I was giving orders. Lewin was to obey *me*, not the Thrallers, and my orders were to drive away *at once*. When nothing seemed to happen, I got so scared that I seemed to be filling the whole van with my orders.

'Thank you,' Lewin said, in a croaking sort of voice. He jerked the van round into Worm Parade and roared down it, away from the ship and the terrible ramps. The swerve sent the van door open with a slam and, to my relief, the body of poor Renick tumbled out into the road.

But everyone else screamed out, 'No! What are you doing?' and clutched their heads. The compulsion was far, far worse if you disobeyed. I felt as if layers of my brain were being peeled off with hot pincers. Neal was crying, like Alectis. Terens was moaning. It hurt so much that I filled the van frantically with more and more orders. Lewin made grinding sounds, deep in his throat, and kept on driving away, with the door flapping and banging.

Palino took his straps off and yelled, 'You're going the wrong way, you damn cariarder!' I couldn't stop him at all. He started to climb into the front seat to take the controls away from Lewin. Alectis and Neal both rose up too and shoved him off Lewin. So Palino gave that up and scrambled for the open flapping door instead. Nobody could do a thing. He just jumped out and went rolling in the road. I didn't see what he did then, because I was too busy giving orders, but Neal says he simply scrambled up and staggered back towards the ship and the ramp.

We drove for another horrible half-mile, and then we must have got out of range. Everything suddenly went easy. It was like when somebody lets go the other end of a rope you're both pulling, and you go over backwards. Wham. And I felt too dim and stunned to move.

'Thank the gods!' I heard Terens more or less howl.

'It's Siglin you should be thanking,' Lewin said. 'Alectis, climb over to the front and shut that door. Then try and raise Holmstad again.'

Neal says the door was too battered to shut. Alectis had to hold it with one hand while he worked the broadcaster with the other. I heard him saying that Holmstad still didn't answer through the roaring and rattling the van made when Lewin put on speed up the long looping gradient of Wormjiot. We hadn't nearly got up to the Saddle, when Terens said, 'It's going! Aren't they quick!' I looked back, still feeling dim and horrible, in time to see the squatting hedgehog rise up inside the clouds again.

'Now you can thank the gods,' Lewin said. 'They didn't think we were worth chasing. Try medium wave, Alectis.' There is an outcrop of ragged rock near the head of Wormjiot. Lewin drove off the road and stopped behind it while Alectis fiddled with knobs.

Instead of getting dance music and cookery hints, Alectis got a voice that fizzed and crackled. 'This is Dragonate Fanejiot, Sveridge South, with an emergency message for all Dragonate units still in action. You are required to make your way to Fanejiot and report there soonest.' It said that about seven times, then it said, 'We can now confirm earlier reports that

Home Nine is in Slaver hands. Here is a list of bases on Home Eight that have been taken by Slavers.' It was a long list. Holmstad came quite early on it, and Ranefell about ten names after that.

Lewin reached across and turned it off. 'Did someone say we slipped up?' he said. 'That was an understatement.'

'Fanejiot is two thousand flaming miles from here!' Terens said. 'With an ocean and who knows how many Slavers in between!'

'Well put,' said Lewin. 'Did Palino's memo block go to the Slavers with him?'

It was lying on the back seat beside Neal. Neal tried to pretend it wasn't, but Alectis turned round and grabbed it as Neal tried to shove it on the floor. I was lying back in my straps, feeling grey and thinking, We could get away now. I'd better lam them all again. But all I did was lie there and watch Neal and Alectis having an angry tug-of-war. Then watch Lewin turn round and pluck the block away from the pair of them.

'Don't be a fool,' he said to Neal. 'I've already erased the recorder. And if I hadn't had Renick and Palino breathing righteously down our necks, I'd never have recorded anything. It goes against the grain to take in children.'

Lewin pressed the *erase* on the memo block and it gave out a satisfied sort of gobble. Neither of the other two said anything, but I could feel Alectis thinking how much he had always hated Palino. Terens was looking down at Wormstow through a field glass and trying not to remember a boy in Cadets with him who had turned heg and given himself up. I felt I wanted to say thank you. But I was too shy to do anything but sit up and look at Wormstow too, between the jags of the rock. Even without a fieldglass, I could see the

131

place throbbing like a broken anthill with all the Slaver troops.

'Getting ready to move out and mop up the countryside,' Terens said.

'Yes, and that's where most people live,' Lewin said. 'Farms and holdings in the hills. What's the quickest way to the Dragon Reserve?'

'There's a track on the right round the next bend,' said Neal. 'Why?'

'Because it's the safest place I can think of,' Lewin said.

Neal and I looked at one another. You didn't need to be heg to tell that Neal was thinking, just as I was, that this was a bit much. They were supposed to help all those people in the holdings. Instead, they thought of the safest place and ran there! So neither of us said that the track was only a bridle path, and we didn't try to warn them not to take the van into the Reserve. We just sat there while Lewin drove it uphill, and then lumping and bumping and rattling up the path. The path gave out in the marshy patch below the Saddle, but Lewin kept grinding and roaring on, throwing up peat in squirts, until we tipped downhill again and bounced down a yellow fellside. We were in the Reserve by then. The ling was growing in lurid green patches, black at the roots, where dragons had burnt it in the mating season. They fight a lot then.

We got some way into the Reserve. The van gave out clanging sounds and smelt bad, but Lewin kept it going by driving on the most level parts. We were in a wide stony scoop, with yellow hills all round, when the smell got worse and the van just stopped. Alectis let go of the door. 'Worms – dragons,' he said, 'don't like machines, I've heard.'

'Now he tells us!' said Terens, and we all got out.

We all looked as if we had been in an accident – I mean, I know we had in a way, but we looked worse than I'd expected: sort of ragged and pale and shivery. Lewin turned his foot on a stone, which made him clutch his chest and swear. Neither of the other two even asked if he was all right. That is the Dragonate way. They just set out walking. Neal and I went with them, thinking of the best place to dodge off up a kyle, so that we could run home and try and warn Mother about the Slavers.

'Where that bog turns into a stream – I'll say when,' Neal was whispering, when a dragon came over the hill into the valley and made straight for us.

'Stand still!' said Alectis. Lewin and Terens each had a gun in their hand without seeming to have moved. Alectis didn't, and he was white.

'They only eat moving prey,' Neal said, because he was sorry for him. 'Make sure not to panic and run and you're fine.'

I was sorry for Alectis too, so I added, 'It's probably only after the van. They love metal.'

Lewin crumpled his face at me and said 'Ah!' for some reason.

The dragon came quite slowly, helping itself with its spread wings and hanging its head rather. It was a bad colour, sort of creamy through the brown-green. I thought it might be one of the sick ones that turn man-eater, and I tried to brace myself and stop feeling so tired and shaky so that I could lam it. But Neal said, 'That's Orm's dragon! You didn't kill it after all!'

It *was* Orm's dragon. By this time, it was near enough for me to see the heat off it quivering the air, and I recognized the gamesome, shrewd look in its eyes. But since it had every reason to hate me, that didn't make me feel much better. It came straight for me too. We all stood like statues. And it came right up to me and bent its neck, and laid its huge brown head on the ling in front of my feet, where it puffed out a sigh that made Lewin cough and gasp another swearword. It had felt me coming, the dragon said, and it was here to say sorry. It hadn't meant to upset me. It had thought it was a game.

That made me feel terrible. 'I'm sorry too,' I said. 'I lost my head. I didn't mean to hurt you. That was Orm's fault.'

Orm was only playing too, the dragon said. Orm called him Huffle, and I could too if I liked. Was he forgiven? He was ashamed.

'Of course I forgive you, Huffle,' I said. 'Do you forgive me?'

Yes. Huffle lifted his head up and went a proper colour at once. Dragons are like people that way.

'Ask him to fetch Orm here,' Lewin said urgently.

I didn't want to see Orm, and Lewin was a coward. 'Ask him yourself,' I said. 'He understands.'

'Yes, but I don't think he'd do it for me,' Lewin said.

'Then, will you fetch Orm for Lewin?' I asked Huffle.

He gave me a cheeky look. Maybe. Presently. He sauntered away past Terens, who moved his head back from Huffle's rattling right wing, looking as if he thought his last hour had come, and went to have a look at the van. He put out a great clawed foot, in a thoughtful sort of way, and tore the loose door off it. Then he tucked the door under his right front foreleg and departed, deliberately slowly, on three legs, helping himself with his wings, so that rocks rattled and flapped all along the valley.

Alectis sat down rather suddenly. But Lewin made him leap up again and help Terens get the broadcaster

134

out of the van before any more dragons found it. They never did get it out. They were still working and waggling at it to get it loose, and Lewin was standing over Neal and me, so that we couldn't sneak off, when we heard that humming kind of whistle that you get from a dragon in flight. We whirled round. The dragon was a big black one, coasting low over the hill opposite and gliding down the valley. They don't often fly high. It came to ground with that grinding of stones and leathery slap of wings closing that always tells you a dragon is landing. It arched its black neck and looked at us disdainfully.

Orm was sitting on its back looking equally disdainful. It was one of those times when Orm looks grave and grand. He sat very upright, with his hair and beard combed straight by the wind of flying, and his big pale eyes hardly looked mad at all. Neal was the only one of us he deigned to notice. 'Good afternoon, Neal Sigridsson,' he said. 'You keep bad company. Dragonate are not human.'

Neal was very angry with Orm. He put my heart in my mouth by saying, quite calmly, 'Then in that case, I'm the only human here.' With that dragon standing glaring! I've been brought up to despise boys, but I think that is a mistake.

To my relief, Orm just grinned. 'That's the way, boy,' he said. 'Not a booby after all, are you?'

Then Lewin took my breath away by going right up to the dragon. He had his gun, of course, but that wouldn't have been much use against a dragon. He went so near that the dragon had to turn its head out of his way. 'We've dropped the charges,' he said. 'And you should never have brought them.'

Orm looked down at him. 'You,' he said, 'know a thing or two.'

135

'I know dragons don't willingly attack humans,' Lewin said. 'I always read up on a case before I hear it.' At this, Orm put on his crazy look and made his mad cackle. 'Stop that!' said Lewin. 'The Slavers have invaded. Wormstow's full of Slaver troops and we need your help. I want to get everyone from the outlying farms into the Reserve and persuade the dragons to protect them. Can you help us do that?'

That took my breath away again, and Neal's too. We did a quick goggle at one another. Perhaps the Dragonate was like it was supposed to be after all!

Orm said, 'Then we'd better get busy,' and slid down from the dragon. He still towered over Lewin. Orm is huge. As soon as he was down, the black dragon lumbered across to the van and started taking it to bits. That brought other dragons coasting whistling in from all sides of the valley, to crunch to earth and hurry to the van too. In seconds, it was surrounded in black and green-brown shapes the size of haybarns. And Orm talked, at the top of his voice, through the sound of metal tearing, and big claws screaming on iron, and wings clapping, and angry grunts when two dragons happened to get hold of the same piece of van. Orm always talks a lot. But this time, he was being particularly garrulous, to give the dragons time to lumber away with their pieces of van, hide them and come back. 'They won't even do what Orm says until they've got their metal,' I whispered to Terens, who got rather impatient with Orm.

Orm said the best place to put people was the high valley at the centre of the Reserve. 'There's an old shedrake with a litter just hatched,' he said. 'No one will get past her when she's feared for her young. I'll speak to her. But the rest are to promise me she's not disturbed.' As for telling everyone at the farms where

136

to come, Orm said, the dragons could do that, provided Lewin could think of a way of sending a message by them. 'You see, most folk can't hear a dragon when it speaks,' he said. 'And some who can hear – ' with a nasty look at me ' – speak back to wound.' He was still very angry with me. I kept on the other side of Terens and Alectis when the dragons all came swooping back.

Terens set the memo block to *repeat* and tapped out an official message from Lewin. Then he tore off page after page with the same thing on it. Orm handed each page to a dragon, saying things like, 'Take this to the fat cow up at Hillfoot.' Or, 'Drop this on young vinegar lady at Crowtop – hard.' Or, 'This is for Dopey at High Jiot, but don't give it her, give it to her youngest husband or they'll never get moving.'

Some of the things he said made me laugh at lot. But it was only when Alectis asked what was so funny and Neal kicked my ankle, that I realized I was the only one who could hear the things Orm said. Each dragon, as it got its page, ran down the valley and took off, showering us with stones from the jump they gave to get higher in the air than usual. Their wings boom when they fly high. Orm took off on the black dragon last of all, saying he would go and warn the she-drake.

Lewin crumpled his face ruefully at the few bits of van remaining, and we set off to walk to the valley ourselves. It was a long way. Over ling slopes and up among boulders in the kyles we trudged, looking up nervously every so often when fat bluish Slaver fliers screamed through the clouds overhead. After a while, our dragons began booming overhead too, seawards to roost. Terens counted them and said every one we had sent seemed to have come back. He said he wished he had wings. It was sunset by the time we reached the valley. By that time, Lewin was bent over, holding his chest and swearing every other step. But everyone was still pretending, in that stupid Dragonate way, that he was all right. We came up on the cliffs, where the kyle winds down to the she-drake's valley, and there was the sunset lighting the sea and the towers of rock out there, and the waves crashing round the rocks, where the young dragons were flying to roost – and Lewin actually pretended to admire the view. 'I knew a place like this on Seven,' he said. 'Except there were trees instead of dragons. I can't get used to the way Eight doesn't have trees.'

He was going to sit down to rest, I think, but Orm came up the kyle just then. Huffle was hulking behind him. 'So you got here at last!' Orm said in his rudest way.

'We have,' said Lewin. 'Now would you mind telling me what you were playing at bringing those charges against Siglin?'

'You should be glad I did. You'd all be in a slaveship now if I hadn't,' Orm said.

'But you weren't to know that, were you?' Terens said.

'Not to speak of risking being charged yourself,' added Lewin.

Orm leant on his hand against Huffle, like you might against a wall. 'She half killed this dragon!' he said. 'That's why! All I did was ask her for a kiss and she screams and lays into poor Huffle. My own daughter, and she tries to kill a dragon! And I thought, Right, my lady, then you're no daughter of mine any more! And I flew Huffle's mother straight into Holmstad and laid charges. I was that angry! My own father tended dragons, and his mother before

138

him. And my daughter tried to kill one! You wonder I was angry!'

'Nobody *told* me!' I said. I had that draining-away feeling again. I was quite glad when Terens took hold of my elbow and said something like, 'Steady, steady!'

'Are you telling the truth?' Neal said.

'I'm sure he is,' Lewin said. 'Your sister has his eyes.'

'Ask Timas,' said Orm. 'He married your mother the year after I did. He can take being bossed about. I can't. I went back to my dragons. But I suppose there's a record of that?' he said challengingly to Lewin.

'And the divorce,' said Lewin. 'Terens looked it up for me. But I expect the Slavers have destroyed it by now.'

'And she never told you?' Orm said to me. He wagged his shaggy eyebrows at me almost forgivingly. 'I'll have a bone to pick with her over that,' he said.

Mother arrived just as we'd all got down into the valley. She looked very indomitable, as she always does on horseback, and all our people were with her, down to both our shepherds. They had carts of clothes and blankets and food. Mother knew the valley as well as Orm did. She used to meet Orm there when she was a girl. She set out for the Reserve as soon as she heard the broadcast about the invasion, and the dragon we sent her met them on the way. That's Mother for you. The rest of the neighbours didn't get there for some hours after that.

I didn't think Mother's face – or Timas's – could hold such a mixture of feelings as they did when they saw Neal and me and the Dragonate men all with Orm. When Orm saw Mother, he folded his arms and grinned. Huffle rested his huge chin on Orm's shoulder, looking interested.

'Here she comes,' Orm said to Huffle. 'Oh, I do love a good quarrel!'

They had one. It was one of the loudest I'd ever heard. Terens took Neal and me away to help look after Lewin. He turned out to have broken some ribs when the blast hit the van, but he wouldn't let anyone look even until I ordered him to. After that, Neal, Alectis and I sat under our haycart and talked, mostly about the irony of Fate. You see, Neal has always secretly wished Fate had given him Orm as a father, and I'm the one that's got Orm. Neal's father is Timas. Alectis says he can see the likeness. We'd both gladly swap. Then Alectis confessed that he'd been hating the Dragonate so much that he was thinking of running away – which is a serious crime. But now the Slavers have come, and there doesn't seem to be much of a Dragonate any more, he feels quite different. He admires Lewin.

Lewin consented to rest while Terens and Mother organized everyone into a makeshift camp in the valley, but he was up and about again the next day, because he said the Slavers were bound to come the day after, when they found the holdings were deserted. The big black she-drake sat in her cave at the head of the kyle, with her infants between her forefeet, watching groups of people rushing round to do what Lewin said, and didn't seem to mind at all. Huffle said she'd been bored and bad-tempered up to then. We made life interesting. Actually that she-drake reminds me of Mother. Both of them made me give them a faithful report of the battle.

I don't think the Slavers knew about the dragons. They just knew that there was a concentration of people in here, and they came straight across the Reserve to get us. As soon as the dragons told Orm they were coming, Lewin had us all out hiding in the hills in their path, except for Mother and Timas and Inga's mother and a few more who had shotguns. They had to stay and guard the little kids in the camp. The rest of us had any weapon we could find. Neal and Alectis had bows and arrows. Inga had her airgun. Donal and most of the farmers had scythes. The shepherds all had their slingshots. I was in the front with Lewin, because I was supposed to stop the effect of the Slavers' collars. Orm was there too, although nobody had ever admitted in so many words that Orm might be heg. All Orm did was to ask the dragons to keep back, because we didn't want *them* enslaved by those collars.

And there they came, a huddle of sheep-like troops, and then another huddle, each one being driven by a cluster of kingly Slavers, with crowns and winking V-shaped collars. And there again we all got that horrible guilty compulsion to come and give ourselves up. But I don't think those collars have any effect on dragons. Half of us were standing up to walk into the Slavers' arms, and I was ordering them as hard as I could not to, when the dragons smelt those golden crowns and collars. There was no holding them. They just whirred down over our heads and took those Slavers to pieces for the metal. Lewin said, 'Ah!' and crumpled his face in a grin like a fiend's. He'd thought the dragons might do that. I think he may really be a genius, like they say Camerati are. But I was so sick at that, and then again at the sight of nice people like Alectis and Yan killing the sheep-like troops, that I'm not going to talk about it any more. Terens says I'm not to go when the Slavers come next. Apparently I broadcast the way I was feeling, just like the Slavers do, and even the dragons felt queasy. The she-drake snorted at that. Mother says, 'Nonsense. Take travel pills and behave as my daughter should.'

Anyway, we have found out how to beat the Slavers. We have no idea what is going on in the other of the Ten Worlds, or even in the rest of Sveridge, but there are fifty more Worm Reserves around the world, and Lewin says there must be stray Dragonate units too who might think of using dragons against Slavers. We want to move out and take over some of the farms again soon. The dragons are having far too much fun with the sheep. They keep flying over with woolly bundles dangling from their claws, watched by a gloomy crowd of everyone's shepherds. 'Green dot,' the shepherds say. 'The brutes are raiding Hightop now.' They are very annoyed with Orm, because Orm just gives his mad cackle and lets the dragons go on.

Orm isn't mad at all. He's afraid of people knowing he's heg — he still won't admit he is. I think that's why he left Mother and Mother doesn't admit she was ever married to him. Not that Mother minds. I get the feeling she and Orm understand one another rather well. But Mother married Donal, you see, after Timas. Donal, and Yan too, have both told me that the fact that I'm heg makes no difference to them — but you should see the way they both look at me! I'm not fooled. I don't blame Orm for being scared stiff Donal would find out he was heg. But I'm not sure I shall ever like Orm, all the same.

I am putting all this down on what is left of Palino's memo block. Lewin wanted me to, in case there is still some History yet to come. He has made his official version on the recorder. I'm leaning the block on

142

Huffle's forefoot. Huffle is my friend now. Leaning on a dragon is the best way to keep warm on a chilly evening like this, when you're forced to camp out in the Reserve. Huffle is letting Lewin lean on him too, beyond Neal, because Lewin's ribs still pain him. There is a lot of leaning-space along the side of a dragon. Orm has just stepped across Huffle's tail, into the light, chortling and rubbing his hands in his most irritating way.

'Your mother's on the warpath,' he says. 'Oh, I do love a good quarrel!'

And here comes Mother, ominously upright, and with her arms folded. It's not Orm she wants. It's Lewin. 'Listen, you,' she says. 'What the dickens is the Dragonate thinking of, beheading hegs all these years? They can't help what they are. And they're the only people who can stand up to the Thrallers.'

Orm is cheated of his quarrel. Lewin looked up, crumpled into the most friendly smile. 'I do so agree with you,' he said. 'I've just said so in my report. And I'd have got your daughter off somehow, you know.'

Orm is cackling like the she-drake's young ones. Mother's mouth is open and I really think that, for once in her life, she has no idea what to say.

The Sage of Theare

There was a world called Theare in which Heaven was very well organized. Everything was so precisely worked out that every god knew his or her exact duties, correct prayers, right times for business, utterly exact character and unmistakable place above or below other gods. This was the case from Great Zond, the King of the Gods, through every god, godlet, deity, minor deity and numen, down to the most immaterial nymph. Even the invisible dragons that lived in the rivers had their invisible lines of demarcation. The universe ran like clockwork. Mankind was not always so regular, but the gods were there to set him right. It had been like this for centuries.

So it was a breach in the very nature of things when, in the middle of the yearly Festival of Water, at which only watery deities were entitled to be present, Great Zond looked up to see Imperion, god of the sun, storming towards him down the halls of Heaven.

'Go away!' cried Zond, aghast.

But Imperion swept on, causing the watery deities gathered there to steam and hiss, and arrived in a wave of heat and warm water at the foot of Zond's high throne.

'Father!' Imperion cried urgently.

A high god like Imperion was entitled to call Zond

Father. Zond did not recall whether or not he was actually Imperion's father. The origins of the gods were not quite so orderly as their present existence. But Zond knew that, son of his or not, Imperion had breached all the rules. 'Abase yourself,' Zond said sternly.

Imperion ignored this command, too. Perhaps this was just as well, since the floor of Heaven was awash already, and steaming. Imperion kept his flaming gaze on Zond. 'Father! The Sage of Dissolution has been born!'

Zond shuddered in the clouds of hot vapour and tried to feel resigned. 'It is written,' he said, 'a Sage shall be born who shall question everything. His questions shall bring down the exquisite order of heaven and cast all the gods into disorder. It is also written –' Here Zond realized that Imperion had made him break the rules too. The correct procedure was for Zond to summon the god of prophecy and have that god consult the Book of Heaven. Then he realized that Imperion *was* the god of prophecy. It was one of his precisely allotted duties. Zond rounded on Imperion. 'What do you mean coming and telling me? You're god of prophecy! Go and look in the Book of Heaven.'

'I already have, Father,' said Imperion. 'I find I prophesied the coming of the Sage of Dissolution when the gods first began. It is written that the Sage shall be born and that I shall not know.'

'Then,' said Zond, scoring a point, 'how is it you're here telling me he *has* been born?'

'The mere fact,' Imperion said, 'that I can come here and interrupt the Water Festival, shows that the Sage has been born. Our Dissolution has obviously begun.'

There was a splash of consternation among the

watery gods. They were gathered down the hall as far as they could get from Imperion, but they had all heard. Zond tried to gather his wits. What with the steam raised by Imperion and the spume of dismay thrown out by the rest, the halls of Heaven were in a state nearer chaos than he had known for millenia. Any more of this, and there would be no need for the Sage to ask questions. 'Leave us,' Zond said to the watery gods. 'Events beyond even my control cause this Festival to be stopped. You will be informed later of any decision I make.' To Zond's dismay, the watery ones hesitated – further evidence of Dissolution. 'I promise,' he said.

The watery ones made up their minds. They left in waves, all except one. This one was Ock, god of all oceans. Ock was equal in status to Imperion and heat did not threaten him. He stayed where he was.

Zond was not pleased. Ock, it always seemed to him, was the least orderly of the gods. He did not know his place. He was as restless and unfathomable as mankind. But, with Dissolution already begun, what could Zond do? 'You have our permission to stay,' he said graciously to Ock, and to Imperion. 'Well, how did you know the Sage was born?'

'I was consulting the Book of Heaven on another matter,' said Imperion, 'and the page opened at my prophecy concerning the Sage of Dissolution. Since it said that I would not know the day and hour when the Sage was born, it followed that he has already been born, or I would not have known. The rest of the prophecy was commendably precise, however. Twenty years from now, he will start questioning Heaven. What shall we do to stop him?'

'I don't see what we can do,' Zond said hopelessly. 'A prophecy is a prophecy.'

'But we must do something!' blazed Imperion. 'I insist! I am a god of order, even more than you are. Think what would happen if the sun went inaccurate! This means more to me than anyone. I want the Sage of Dissolution found and killed before he can ask questions.'

Zond was shocked. 'I can't do that! If the prophecy says he has to ask questions, then he has to ask them.'

Here Ock approached. 'Every prophecy has a loophole,' he said.

'Of course,' snapped Imperion. 'I can see the loophole as well as you. I'm taking advantage of the disorder caused by the birth of the Sage to ask Great Zond to kill him and overthrow the prophecy. Thus restoring order.'

'Logic-chopping is not what I meant,' said Ock.

The two gods faced one another. Steam from Ock suffused Imperion and then rained back on Ock, as regularly as breathing. 'What did you mean, then?' said Imperion.

'The prophecy,' said Ock, 'does not appear to say which world the Sage will ask his questions in. There are many other worlds. Mankind calls them if-worlds, meaning that they were once the same world as Theare, but split off and went their own way after each doubtful event in history. Each if-world has its own Heaven. There must be one world in which the gods are not as orderly as we are here. Let the Sage be put in that world. Let him ask his predestined questions there.'

'Good idea!' Zond clapped his hands in relief, causing untoward tempests in all Theare. 'Agreed, Imperion?'

'Yes,' said Imperion. He flamed with relief. And, being unguarded, he at once became prophetic. 'But

I must warn you,' he said, 'that strange things happen when destiny is tampered with.'

'Strange things maybe, but never disorderly,' Zond asserted. He called the watery gods back and, with them, every god in Theare. He told them that an infant had just been born who was destined to spread Dissolution, and he ordered each one of them to search the ends of the earth for this child. ('The ends of the earth' was a legal formula. Zond did not believe that Theare was flat. But the expression had been unchanged for centuries, just like the rest of Heaven. It meant 'Look everywhere.')

The whole of Heaven looked high and low. Nymphs and godlets scanned mountains, caves and woods. Household gods peered into cradles. Watery gods searched beaches, banks and margins. The goddess of love went deeply into her records, to find who the Sage's parents might be. The invisible dragons swam to look inside barges and houseboats. Since there was a god for everything in Theare, nowhere was missed, nothing was omitted. Imperion searched harder than any, blazing into every nook and crevice on one side of the world, and exhorting the moon goddess to do the same on the other side.

And nobody found the Sage. There were one or two false alarms, such as when a household goddess reported an infant that never stopped crying. This baby, she said, was driving her up the wall and, if this was not Dissolution, she would like to know what was. There were also several reports of infants born with teeth, or six fingers, or suchlike strangeness. But, in each case, Zond was able to prove that the child had nothing to do with Dissolution. After a month, it became clear that the infant Sage was not going to be found.

Imperion was in despair, for, as he had told Zond, order meant more to him than to any other god. He became so worried that he was actually causing the sun to lose heat. At length, the goddess of love advised him to go off and relax with a mortal woman before he brought about Dissolution himself. Imperion saw she was right. He went down to visit the human woman he had loved for some years. It was established custom for gods to love mortals. Some visited their loves in all sorts of fanciful shapes, and some had many loves at once. But Imperion was both honest and faithful. He never visited Nestara as anything but a handsome man, and he loved her devotedly. Three years ago, she had borne him a son, whom Imperion loved almost as much as he loved Nestara. Before the Sage was born to trouble him, Imperion had been trying to bend the rules of Heaven a little, to get his son approved as a god too.

The child's name was Thasper. As Imperion descended to earth, he could see Thasper digging in some sand outside Nestara's house – a beautiful child, fair-haired and blue-eyed. Imperion wondered fondly if Thasper was talking properly yet. Nestara had been worried about how slow he was learning to speak.

Imperion alighted beside his son. 'Hello, Thasper. What are you digging so busily?'

Instead of answering, Thasper raised his golden head and shouted. 'Mum!' he yelled. 'Why does it go bright when Dad comes?'

All Imperion's pleasure vanished. Of course no one could ask questions until he had learned to speak. But it would be too cruel if his own son turned out to be the Sage of Dissolution. 'Why shouldn't it go bright?' he said defensively.

149

Thasper scowled up at him. 'I want to know. *Why* does it?'

'Perhaps because you feel happy to see me,' Imperion suggested.'

'I'm not happy,' Thasper said. His lower lip came out. Tears filled his big blue eyes. 'Why does it go bright? I want to *know*. Mum! I'm not happy!'

Nestara came racing out of the house, almost too concerned to smile at Imperion. 'Thasper love, what's the matter?'

'I want to *know*!' wailed Thasper.

'What do you want to know? I've never known such an inquiring mind,' Nestara said proudly to Imperion, as she picked Thasper up. 'That's why he was so slow talking. He wouldn't speak until he'd found out how to ask questions. And if you don't give him an exact answer, he'll cry for hours.'

'When did he first start asking questions?' Imperion inquired tensely.

'About a month ago,' said Nestara.

This made Imperion truly miserable, but he concealed it. It was clear to him that Thasper was indeed the Sage of Dissolution and he was going to have to take him away to another world. He smiled and said, 'My love, I have wonderful news for you. Thasper has been accepted as a god. Great Zond himself will have him as cupbearer.'

'Oh not now!' cried Nestara. 'He's so little!'

She made numerous other objections too. But, in the end, she let Imperion take Thasper. After all, what better future could there be for a child? She put Thasper into Imperion's arms with all sorts of anxious advice about what he ate and when he went to bed. Imperion kissed her goodbye, heavy-hearted. He was not a god of deception. He knew he dared not see her again for fear he told her the truth.

Then, with Thasper in his arms, Imperion went up to the middle-regions below Heaven, to look for another world.

Thasper looked down with interest at the great blue curve of the world. 'Why – ?' he began.

Imperion hastily enclosed him in a sphere of forgetfulness. He could not afford to let Thasper ask things here. Questions that spread Dissolution on earth would have an even more powerful effect in the middle-region. The sphere was a silver globe, neither transparent nor opaque. In it, Thasper would stay seemingly asleep, not moving and not growing, until the sphere was opened. With the child thus safe, Imperion hung the sphere from one shoulder and stepped into the next-door world.

He went from world to world. He was pleased to find there were an almost infinite number of them, for the choice proved supremely difficult. Some worlds were so disorderly that he shrank from leaving Thasper in them. In some, the gods resented Imperion's intrusion and shouted at him to be off. In others, it was mankind that was resentful. One world he came to was so rational that, to his horror, he found the gods were dead. There were many others he thought might do, until he let the spirit of prophecy blow through him, and in each case this told him that harm would come to Thasper here. But at last he found a good world. It seemed calm and elegant. The few gods there seemed civilized but casual. Indeed, Imperion was a little puzzled to find that these gods seemed to share quite a lot of their power with mankind. But mankind did not seem to abuse this power, and the spirit of prophecy assured him that, if

151

he left Thasper here inside his sphere of forgetfulness, it would be opened by someone who would treat the boy well.

Imperion put the sphere down in a wood and sped back to Theare, heartily relieved. There, he reported what he had done to Zond, and all Heaven rejoiced. Imperion made sure that Nestara married a very rich man who gave her not only wealth and happiness but plenty of children to replace Thasper. Then, a little sadly, he went back to the ordered life of Heaven. The exquisite organization of Theare went on untroubled by Dissolution.

Seven years passed.

All that while, Thasper knew nothing and remained three years old. Then one day, the sphere of forgetfulness fell in two halves and he blinked in sunlight somewhat less golden than he had known.

'So that's what was causing all the disturbance,' a tall man murmured.

'Poor little soul!' said a lady.

There was a wood around Thasper, and people standing in it looking at him, but, as far as Thasper knew, nothing had happened since he soared to the middle-region with his father. He went on with the question he had been in the middle of asking. 'Why is the world round?' he said.

'Interesting question,' said the tall man. 'The answer usually given is because the corners wore off spinning around the sun. But it could be designed to make us end where we began.'

'Sir, you'll muddle him, talking like that,' said another lady. 'He's only little.'

'No, he's interested,' said another man. 'Look at him.'

Thasper was indeed interested. He approved of the

152

tall man. He was a little puzzled about where he had come from, but he supposed the tall man must have been put there because he answered questions better than Imperion. He wondered where Imperion had got to. 'Why aren't you my Dad?' he asked the tall man.

'Another most penetrating question,' said the tall man. 'Because, as far as we can find out, your father lives in another world. Tell me your name.'

This was another point in the tall man's favour. Thasper never answered questions: he only asked them. But this was a command. The tall man understood Thasper. 'Thasper,' Thasper answered obediently.

'He's sweet!' said the first lady. 'I want to adopt him.' To which the other ladies gathered around most heartily agreed.

'Impossible,' said the tall man. His tone was mild as milk and rock firm. The ladies were reduced to begging to be able to look after Thasper for a day, then. An hour. 'No,' the tall man said mildly. 'He must go back at once.' At which all the ladies cried out that Thasper might be in great danger in his own home. The tall man said, 'I shall take care of that, of course.' Then he stretched out a hand and pulled Thasper up. 'Come along, Thasper.'

As soon as Thasper was out of it, the two halves of the sphere vanished. One of the ladies took his other hand and he was led away, first on a jiggly ride, which he much enjoyed, and then into a huge house, where there was a very perplexing room. In this room, Thasper sat in a five-pointed star and pictures kept appearing around him. People kept shaking their heads. 'No, not that world either.' The tall man answered all Thasper's questions, and Thasper was

153

too interested even to be annoyed when they would not allow him anything to eat.

'Why not?' he said.

'Because, just by being here, you are causing the world to jolt about,' the tall man explained. 'If you put food inside you, food is a heavy part of this world, and it might jolt you to pieces.'

Soon after that, a new picture appeared. Everyone said 'Ah!' and the tall man said. 'So it's Theare!' He looked at Thasper in a surprised way. 'You must have struck someone as disorderly,' he said. Then he looked at the picture again, in a lazy, careful kind of way. 'No disorder,' he said. 'No danger. Come with me.'

He took Thasper's hand again and led him into the picture. As he did so, Thasper's hair turned much darker. 'A simple precaution,' the tall man murmured, a little apologetically, but Thasper did not even notice. He was not aware what colour his hair had been to start with, and besides, he was taken up with surprise at how fast they were going. They whizzed into a city, and stopped abruptly. It was a good house, just on the edge of a poorer district. 'Here is someone who will do,' the tall man said, and he knocked at the door.

A sad-looking lady opened the door.

'I beg your pardon, madam,' said the tall man, 'Have you by any chance lost a small boy?'

'Yes,' said the lady. 'But this isn't –' She blinked. 'Yes it *is* !' she cried out. 'Oh Thasper! How could you run off like that? Thank you so much, sir.' But the tall man had gone.

The lady's name was Alina Altun, and she was so convinced that she was Thasper's mother that Thasper was soon convinced too. He settled in happily with her and her husband, who was a doctor,

154

hard-working but not very rich. Thasper soon forgot the tall man, Imperion and Nestara. Sometimes it did puzzle him – and his new mother too – that when she showed him off to her friends she always felt bound to say, 'This is Badien, but we always call him Thasper.' Thanks to the tall man, none of them ever knew that the real Badien had wandered away the day Thasper came and fell in the river, where an invisible dragon ate him.

If Thasper had remembered the tall man, he might also have wondered why his arrival seemed to start Dr Altun on the road to prosperity. The people in the poorer district nearby suddenly discovered what a good doctor Dr Altun was, and how little he charged. Alina was shortly able to afford to send Thasper to a very good school, where Thasper often exasperated his teachers by his many questions. He had, as his new mother often proudly said, a most inquiring mind. Although he learned quicker than most the Ten First Lessons and the Nine Graces of Childhood, his teachers were nevertheless often annoyed enough to snap, 'Oh, go and ask an invisible dragon!' which is what people in Theare often said when they thought they were being pestered.

Thasper did, with difficulty, gradually cure himself of his habit of never answering questions. But he always preferred asking to answering. At home, he asked questions all the time: 'Why does the kitchen god go and report to Heaven once a year? Is it so I can steal biscuits? Why are invisible dragons? Is there a god for everything? Why is there a god for everything? If the gods make people ill, how can Dad cure them? Why must I have a baby brother or sister?'

Alina Altun was a good mother. She most diligently answered all these questions, including the last. She

155

told Thasper how babies were made, ending her account with, 'Then, if the gods bless my womb, a baby will come.' She was a devout person.

'I don't want you to be blessed!' Thasper said, resorting to a statement, which he only did when he was strongly moved.

He seemed to have no choice in the matter. By the time he was ten years old, the gods had thought fit to bless him with two brothers and two sisters. In Thasper's opinion, they were, as blessings, very low grade. They were just too young to be any use. 'Why can't they be the same age as me?' he demanded, many times. He began to bear the gods a small but definite grudge about this.

Dr Altun continued to prosper and his earnings more than kept pace with his family. Alina employed a nursemaid, a cook, and a number of rather impermanent houseboys. It was one of these houseboys who, when Thasper was eleven, shyly presented Thasper with a folded square of paper. Wondering, Thasper unfolded it. It gave him a curious feeling to touch, as if the paper was vibrating a little in his fingers. It also gave out a very strong warning that he was not to mention it to anybody. It said:

> Dear Thasper,
> Your situation is an odd one. Make sure that you call me at the moment when you come face to face with yourself. I shall be watching and I will come at once.
> Yrs,
Chrestomanci

Since Thasper by now had not the slightest recollection of his early life, this letter puzzled him extremely.

156

He knew he was not supposed to tell anyone about it, but he also knew that this did not include the houseboy. With the letter in his hand, he hurried after the houseboy to the kitchen.

He was stopped at the head of the kitchen stairs by a tremendous smashing of china from below. This was followed immediately by the cook's voice raised in nonstop abuse. Thasper knew it was no good trying to go into the kitchen. The houseboy – who went by the odd name of Cat – was in the process of getting fired, like all the other houseboys before him. He had better go and wait for Cat outside the back door. Thasper looked at the letter in his hand. As he did so, his fingers tingled. The letter vanished.

'It's gone!' he exclaimed, showing by this statement how astonished he was. He never could account for what he did next. Instead of going to wait for the houseboy, he ran to the living-room, intending to tell his mother about it, in spite of the warning. 'Do you know what?' he began. He had invented this meaningless question so that he could tell people things and still make it into an enquiry. 'Do you know what?' Alina looked up. Thasper, though he fully intended to tell her about the mysterious letter, found himself saying, 'The cook's just sacked the new houseboy.'

'Oh bother!' said Alina. 'I shall have to find another one now.'

Annoyed with himself, Thasper tried to tell her again. 'Do you know what? I'm surprised the cook doesn't sack the kitchen god too.'

'Hush dear. Don't talk about the gods that way!' said the devout lady.

By this time, the houseboy had left and Thasper lost the urge to tell anyone about the letter. It remained with him as his own personal exciting secret. He

157

thought of it as The Letter From A Person Unknown. He sometimes whispered the strange name of The Person Unknown to himself when no one could hear. But nothing ever happened, even when he said the name out loud. He gave up doing that after a while. He had other things to think about. He became fascinated by Rules, Laws and Systems.

Rules and Systems were an important part of the life of mankind in Theare. It stood to reason, with Heaven so well organized. People codified all behaviour into things like the Seven Subtle Politenesses, or the Hundred Roads to Godliness. Thasper had been taught these things from the time he was three years old. He was accustomed to hearing Alina argue the niceties of the Seventy-Two Household Laws with her friends. Now Thasper suddenly discovered for himself that all Rules made a magnificent framework for one's mind to clamber about in. He made lists of rules, and refinements on rules, and possible ways of doing the opposite of what the rules said while still keeping the rules. He invented new codes of rules. He filled books and made charts. He invented games with huge and complicated rules, and played them with his friends. Onlookers found these games both rough and muddled, but Thasper and his friends revelled in them. The best moment in any games was when somebody stopped playing and shouted, 'I've thought of a new rule!'

This obsession with rules lasted until Thasper was fifteen. He was walking home from school one day, thinking over a list of rules for Twenty Fashionable Hairstyles. From this, it will be seen that Thasper was noticing girls, though none of the girls had so far seemed to notice him. And he was thinking which girl

158

should wear which hairstyle, when his attention was caught by words chalked on the wall:

IF RULES MAKE A FRAMEWORK FOR THE MIND TO CLIMB ABOUT IN, WHY SHOULD THE MIND NOT CLIMB RIGHT OUT, SAYS THE SAGE OF DISSOLUTION.

That same day, there was consternation again in Heaven. Zond summoned all the high gods to his throne. 'The Sage of Dissolution has started to preach,' he announced direfully. 'Imperion, I thought you got rid of him.'

'I thought I did,' Imperion said. He was even more appalled than Zond. If the Sage had started to preach, it meant that Imperion had got rid of Thasper and deprived himself of Nestara quite unnecessarily. 'I must have been mistaken,' he admitted.

Here Ock spoke up, steaming gently. 'Father Zond,' he said, 'may I respectfully suggest that you deal with the Sage yourself, so that there will be no mistake this time?'

'That was just what I was about to suggest,' Zond said gratefully. 'Are you all agreed?'

All the gods agreed. They were too used to order to do otherwise.

As for Thasper, he was staring at the chalked words, shivering to the soles of his sandals. What was this? Who was using his own private thoughts about rules? Who was this Sage of Dissolution? Thasper was ashamed. He, who was so good at asking questions, had never thought of asking this one. Why should one's mind not climb right out of the rules, after all?

He went home and asked his parents about the Sage of Dissolution. He fully expected them to know. He was quite agitated when they did not. But they had a

159

neighbour, who sent Thasper to another neighbour, who had a friend, who, when Thasper finally found his house, said he had heard that the Sage was a clever young man who made a living by mocking the gods.

The next day, someone had washed the words off. But the day after that, a badly printed poster appeared on the same wall. THE SAGE OF DISSOLUTION ASKS BY WHOSE ORDER IS ORDER ANYWAY?? COME TO SMALL UNCTION SUBLIME CONCERT HALL TONITE 6.30.

At 6.20, Thasper was having supper. At 6.24, he made up his mind and left the table. At 6.32, he arrived panting at Small Unction Hall. It proved to be a small shabby building quite near where he lived. Nobody was there. As far as Thasper could gather from the grumpy caretaker, the meeting had been the night before. Thasper turned away, deeply disappointed. Who ordered the order was a question he now longed to know the answer to. It was deep. He had a notion that the man who called himself the Sage of Dissolution was truly brilliant.

By way of feeding his own disappointment, he went to school the next day by a route which took him past the Small Unction Concert Hall. It had burnt down in the night. There were only blackened brick walls left. When he got to school, a number of people were talking about it. They said it had burst into flames just before 7.00 the night before.

'Did you know,' Thasper said, 'that the Sage of Dissolution was there the day before yesterday?'

That was how he discovered he was not the only one interested in the Sage. Half his class were admirers of Dissolution. That, too, was when the girls deigned to notice him. 'He's amazing about the gods,' one girl told him. 'No one ever asked questions like that before.' Most of the class, however, girls and boys alike, only knew a little more than Thasper, and most of what they knew was second-hand. But a boy showed him a carefully cut-out newspaper article in which a well-known scholar discussed what he called 'The so-called Doctrine of Dissolution'. It said, long-windedly, that the Sage and his followers were rude to the gods and against all the rules. It did not tell Thasper much, but it was something. He saw, rather ruefully, that his obsession with rules had been quite wrong-headed and had, into the bargain, caused him to fall behind the rest of his class in learning of this wonderful new Doctrine. He became a Disciple of Dissolution on the spot. He joined the rest of his class in finding out all they could about the Sage. He went round with them, writing up on walls DISSOLUTION RULES OK.

For a long while after that, the only thing any of Thasper's class could learn of the Sage were scraps of questions chalked on walls and quickly rubbed out. WHAT NEED OF PRAYER? WHY SHOULD THERE BE A HUNDRED ROADS TO GODLINESS, NOT MORE OR LESS? DO WE CLIMB ANYWHERE ON THE STEPS TO HEAVEN? WHAT IS PERFECTION: A PROCESS OR A STATE? WHEN WE CLIMB TO PERFECTION IS THIS A MATTER FOR THE GODS?

Thasper obsessively wrote all these sayings down. He was obsessed again, he admitted, but this time it was in a new way. He was thinking, thinking. At first, he thought simply of clever questions to ask the Sage. He strained to find questions no one had asked before. But in the process, his mind seemed to loosen, and shortly he was thinking of how the Sage might answer his questions. He considered order and rules and Heaven, and it came to him that there was a reason behind all the brilliant questions the Sage asked. He felt light-headed with thinking.

The reason behind the Sage's questions came to him the morning he was shaving for the first time. He thought, *The gods need human beings in order to be gods!* Blinded with this revelation, Thasper stared into the mirror at his own face half covered with white foam. Without humans believing in them, gods were nothing! The order of Heaven, the rules and codes of earth, were all only there because of people! It was transcendent. As Thasper stared, the letter from the Unknown came into his mind. 'Is this being face to face with myself?' he said. But he was not sure. And he became sure that when the time came, he would not have to wonder.

Then it came to him that the Unknown Chrestomanci was almost certainly the Sage himself. He was thrilled. The Sage was taking a special mysterious interest in one teenage boy, Thasper Altun. The vanishing letter exactly fitted the elusive Sage.

The Sage continued elusive. The next firm news of him was a newspaper report of the Celestial Gallery being struck by lightning. The roof of the building collapsed, said the report, 'only seconds after the young man known as the Sage of Dissolution had delivered another of his anguished and self-doubting homilies and left the building with his disciples.'

'He's not self-doubting,' Thasper said to himself. 'He knows about the gods. If *I* know, then *he* certainly does.'

He and his classmates went on a pilgrimage to the ruined gallery. It was a better building than Small Unction Hall. It seemed the Sage was going up in the world.

Then there was enormous excitement. One of the girls found a small advertisement in a paper. The Sage was to deliver another lecture, in the huge Kingdom of Splendour Hall. He had gone up in the world again. Thasper and his friends dressed in their best and went there in a body. But it seemed as if the time for the lecture had been printed wrong. The lecture was just over. People were streaming away from the Hall, looking disappointed.

Thasper and his friends were still in the street when the Hall blew up. They were lucky not to be hurt. The Police said it was a bomb. Thasper and his friends helped drag injured people clear of the blazing Hall. It was exciting, but it was not the Sage.

By now, Thasper knew he would never be happy until he had found the Sage. He told himself that he had to know if the reason behind the Sage's questions was the one he thought. But it was more than that. Thasper was convinced that his fate was linked to the Sage's. He was certain the Sage *wanted* Thasper to find him.

But there was now a strong rumour in school and around town that the Sage had had enough of lectures and bomb attacks. He had retired to write a book. It was to be called *Questions of Dissolution*. Rumour also had it that the Sage was in lodgings somewhere near the Road of the Four Lions.

Thasper went to the Road of the Four Lions. There he was shameless. He knocked on doors and questioned passers-by. He was told several times to go and ask an invisible dragon, but he took no notice. He went on asking until someone told him that Mrs Tunap at 403 might know. Thasper knocked at 403, with his heart thumping.

Mrs Tunap was a rather prim lady in a green turban. 'I'm afraid not, dear,' she said. 'I'm new here.' But before Thasper's heart could sink too far, she added, 'But the people before me had a lodger. A very quiet gentleman. He left just before I came.'

'Did he leave an address?' Thasper asked, holding his breath.

Mrs Tunap consulted an old envelope pinned to the wall in her hall. 'It says here, "Lodger gone to Golden Heart Square", dear.'

But in Golden Heart Square, a young gentleman who might have been the Sage had only looked at a room and gone. After that, Thasper had to go home. The Altuns were not used to teenagers and they worried about Thasper suddenly wanting to be out every evening.

Oddly enough, No. 403 Road of the Four Lions burnt down that night.

Thasper saw clearly that assassins were after the Sage as well as he was. He became more obsessed with finding him than ever. He knew he could rescue the Sage if he caught him before the assassins did. He did not blame the Sage for moving about all the time.

Move about the Sage certainly did. Rumour had him next in Partridge Pleasaunce Street. When Thasper tracked him there, he found the Sage had moved to Fauntel Square. From Fauntel Square, the Sage seemed to move to Strong Wind Boulevard, and then to a poorer house in Station Street. There were many places after that. By this time, Thasper had developed a nose, a sixth sense, for where the Sage might be. A word, a mere hint about a quiet lodger, and Thasper was off, knocking on doors, questioning people, being told to ask an invisible dragon, and bewildering his parents by the way he kept rushing off every evening. But, no matter how quickly Thasper acted on the latest hint, the Sage had always just left.

And Thasper, in most cases, was only just ahead of the assassins. Houses caught fire or blew up sometimes when he was still in the same street.

At last he was down to a very poor hint, which might or might not lead to New Unicorn Street. Thasper went there, wishing he did not have to spend all day at school. The Sage could move about as he pleased, and Thasper was tied down all day. No wonder he kept missing him. But he had high hopes of New Unicorn Street. It was the poor kind of place that the Sage had been favouring lately.

Alas for his hopes. The fat woman who opened the door laughed rudely in Thasper's face. 'Don't bother me, son! Go and ask an invisible dragon!' And she slammed the door again.

Thasper stood in the street, keenly humiliated. And not even a hint of where to look next. Awful suspicions rose in his mind: he was making a fool of himself; he had set himself a wild goose chase; the Sage did not exist. In order not to think of these things, he gave way to anger. 'All right!' he shouted at the shut door. 'I *will* ask an invisible dragon! So there!' And, carried by his anger, he ran down to the river and out across the nearest bridge.

He stopped in the middle of the bridge, leaning on the parapet, and knew he was making an utter fool of himself. There were no such things as invisible dragons. He was sure of that. But he was still in the grip of his obsession, and this was something he had set himself to do now. Even so, if there had been anyone about near the bridge, Thasper would have gone away. But it was deserted. Feeling an utter fool, he made the prayer-sign to Ock, Ruler of Oceans – for Ock was the god in charge of all things to do with water – but he made the sign secretly, down under

165

the parapet, so there was no chance of anyone seeing. Then he said, almost in a whisper, 'Is there an invisible dragon here? I've got something to ask you.'

Drops of water whirled over him. Something wetly fanned his face. He heard the something whirring. He turned his face that way and saw three blots of wet in a line along the parapet, each about two feet apart and each the size of two of his hands spread out together. Odder still, water was dripping out of nowhere all along the parapet, for a distance about twice as long as Thasper was tall.

Thasper laughed uneasily. 'I'm imagining a dragon,' he said. 'If there was a dragon, those splotches would be the places where its body rests. Water dragons have no feet. And the length of the wetness suggests I must be imagining it about eleven feet long.'

'I am fourteen feet long,' said a voice out of nowhere. It was rather too near Thasper's face for comfort and blew fog at him. He drew back. 'Make haste, child-of-a-god,' said the voice. 'What did you want to ask me?'

'I – I – I – ' stammered Thasper. It was not just that he was scared. This was a body-blow. It messed up utterly his notions about gods needing men to believe in them. But he pulled himself together. His voice only cracked a little as he said, 'I'm looking for the Sage of Dissolution. Do you know where he is?'

The dragon laughed. It was a peculiar noise, like one of those water-warblers people make bird noises with. 'I'm afraid I can't tell you precisely where the Sage is,' the voice out of nowhere said. 'You have to find him for yourself. Think about it, child-of-a-god. You must have noticed there's a pattern.'

'Too right, there's a pattern!' Thasper said.

166

'Everywhere he goes, I just miss him, and then the place catches fire!'

'That too,' said the dragon. 'But there's a pattern to his lodgings too. Look for it. That's all I can tell you, child-of-a-god. Any other questions?'

'No – for a wonder,' Thasper said. 'Thanks very much.'

'You're welcome,' said the invisible dragon. 'People are always telling one another to ask us, and hardly anyone does. I'll see you again.' Watery air whirled in Thasper's face. He leaned over the parapet and saw one prolonged clean splash in the river, and silver bubbles coming up. Then nothing. He was surprised to find his legs were shaking.

He steadied his knees and tramped home. He went to his room and, before he did anything else, he acted on a superstitious impulse he had not thought he had in him, and took down the household god Alina insisted he keep in a niche over his bed. He put it carefully outside in the passage. Then he got out a map of the town and some red stickers and plotted out all the places where he had just missed the Sage. The result had him dancing with excitement. The dragon was right. There was a pattern. The Sage had started in good lodgings at the better end of town. Then he had gradually moved to poorer places, but he had moved in a curve, down to the station and back towards the better part again. Now, the Altun's house was just on the edge of the poorer part. The Sage was *coming this way*! New Unicorn Street had not been so far away. The next place should be nearer still. Thasper had only to look for a house on fire.

It was getting dark by then. Thasper threw his curtains back and leaned out of his window to look at

167

the poorer streets. And there it was! There was a red and orange flicker to the left – in Harvest Moon Street, by the look of it. Thasper laughed aloud. He was actually grateful to the assassins!

He raced downstairs and out of the house. The anxious questions of parents and the yells of brothers and sisters followed him, but he slammed the door on them. Two minutes' running brought him to the scene of the fire. The street was a mad flicker of dark figures. People were piling furniture in the road. Some more people were helping a dazed woman in a crooked brown turban into a singed armchair.

'Didn't you have a lodger as well?' someone asked her anxiously.

The woman kept trying to straighten her turban. It was all she could really think of. 'He didn't stay,' she said. 'I think he may be down at the Half Moon now.'

Thasper waited for no more. He went pelting down the street. The Half Moon was an inn on the corner of the same road. Most of the people who usually drank there must have been up the street, helping rescue furniture, but there was a dim light inside, enough to show a white notice in the window. ROOMS, it said.

Thasper burst inside. The barman was on a stool by the window craning to watch the house burn. He did not look at Thasper. 'Where's your lodger?' gasped Thasper. 'I've got a message. Urgent.'

The barman did not turn round. 'Upstairs, first on the left,' he said. 'The roof's caught. They'll have to act quick to save the house on either side.'

Thasper heard him say this as he bounded upstairs. He turned left. He gave the briefest of knocks on the door there, flung it open, and rushed in.

The room was empty. The light was on, and it

168

showed a stark bed, a stained table with an empty mug and some sheets of paper on it, and a fireplace with a mirror over it. Beside the fireplace, another door was just swinging shut. Obviously somebody had just that moment gone through it. Thasper bounded towards that door. But he was checked, for just a second, by seeing himself in the mirror over the fireplace. He had not meant to pause. But some trick of the mirror, which was old and brown and speckled, made his reflection look for a moment a great deal older. He looked easily over twenty. He looked –

He remembered the Letter from the Unknown. This was the time. He knew it was. He was about to meet the Sage. He had only to call him. Thasper went towards the still gently swinging door. He hesitated. The Letter had said call at once. Knowing the Sage was just beyond the door, Thasper pushed it open a fraction and held it so with his fingers. He was full of doubts. He thought, Do I really believe the gods need people? Am I so sure? What shall I say to the Sage after all? He let the door slip shut again.

'Chrestomanci,' he said, miserably.

There was a *whoosh* of displaced air behind him. It buffeted Thasper half around. He stared. A tall man was standing by the stark bed. He was a most extraordinary figure in a long black robe, with what seemed to be yellow comets embroidered on it. The inside of the robe, swirling in the air, showed yellow, with black comets on it. The tall man had a very smooth dark head, very bright dark eyes and, on his feet, what seemed to be red bedroom slippers.

'Thank goodness,' said this outlandish person. 'For a moment, I was afraid you would go through that door.'

The voice brought memory back to Thasper. 'You

brought me home through a picture when I was little,' he said. 'Are you Chrestomanci?'

'Yes,' said the tall outlandish man. 'And you are Thasper. And now we must both leave before this building catches fire.'

He took hold of Thasper's arm and towed him to the door which led to the stairs. As soon as he pushed the door open, thick smoke rolled in, filled with harsh crackling. It was clear that the inn was on fire already. Chrestomanci clapped the door shut again. The smoke set both of them coughing, Chrestomanci so violently that Thasper was afraid he would choke. He pulled both of them back into the middle by the room. By now, smoke was twining up between the bare boards of the floor, causing Chrestomanci to cough again.

'This would happen just as I had gone to bed with flu!' he said, when he could speak. 'Such is life. These orderly gods of yours leave us no choice.' He crossed the smoking floor and pushed open the door by the fireplace.

It opened on to blank space. Thasper gave a yelp of horror.

'Precisely,' coughed Chrestomanci. 'You were intended to crash to your death.'

'Can't we jump to the ground?' Thasper suggested.

Chrestomanci shook his smooth head. 'Not after they've done this to it. No. We'll have to carry the fight to them and go and visit the gods instead. Will you be kind enough to lend me your turban before we go?' Thasper stared at this odd request. 'I would like to use it as a belt,' Chrestomanci croaked. 'The way to Heaven may be a little cold, and I only have pajamas under my dressing-gown.'

The striped undergarments Chrestomanci was

wearing did look a little thin. Thasper slowly unwound his turban. To go before gods bareheaded was probably no worse than going in nightclothes, he supposed. Besides, he did not believe there were any gods. He handed the turban over. Chrestomanci tied the length of pale blue cloth around his black and yellow gown and seemed to feel more comfortable. 'Now hang on to me,' he said, 'and you'll be all right.' He took Thasper's arm again and walked up into the sky, dragging Thasper with him.

For a while, Thasper was too stunned to speak. He could only marvel at the way they were treading up the sky as if there were invisible stairs in it. Chrestomanci was doing it in the most matter of fact way, coughing from time to time, and shivering a little, but keeping very tight hold of Thasper nevertheless. In no time, the town was a clutter of prettily lit dolls' houses below, with two red blots where two of them were burning. The stars were unwinding about them, above and below, as they had already climbed above some of them.

'It's a long climb to Heaven,' Chrestomanci observed. 'Is there anything you'd like to know on the way?'

'Yes,' said Thasper. 'Did you say the gods were trying to kill me?'

'They are trying to eliminate the Sage of Dissolution,' said Chrestomanci, 'which they may not realize is the same thing. You see, you are the Sage.'

'But I'm not!' Thasper insisted. 'The Sage is a lot older than me, and he asks questions I never even thought of until I heard of him.'

'Ah yes,' said Chrestomanci. 'I'm afraid there is an awful circularity to this. It's the fault of whoever tried to put you away as a small child. As far as I can work

171

out, you stayed three years old for seven years – until you were making such a disturbance in our world that we had to find you and let you out. But in this world of Theare, highly organized and fixed as it is, the prophecy stated that you would begin preaching Dissolution at the age of twenty-three, or at least in this very year. Therefore the preaching had to begin this year. You did not need to appear. Did you ever speak to anyone who had actually heard the Sage preach?'

'No,' said Thasper. 'Come to think of it.'

'Nobody did,' said Chrestomanci. 'You started in a small way anyway. First you wrote a book, which no one paid much heed to –'

'No, that's wrong,' objected Thasper. 'He – I – er, the Sage was writing a book *after* the preaching.'

'But don't you see,' said Chrestomanci, 'because you were back in Theare by then, the facts had to try to catch you up. They did this by running backwards until it was possible for you to arrive where you were supposed to be. Which was in that room in the inn there, at the start of your career. I suppose you are just old enough to start by now. And I suspect our celestial friends up here tumbled to this belatedly and tried to finish you off. It wouldn't have done them any good, as I shall shortly tell them.' He began coughing again. They had climbed to where it was bitterly cold.

By this time, the world was a dark arch below them. Thasper could see the blush of the sun, beginning to show underneath the world. They climbed on. The light grew. The sun appeared, a huge brightness in the distance underneath. A dim memory came again to Thasper. He struggled to believe that none of this was true, and he did not succeed.

'How do you know all this?' he asked bluntly.

172

'Have you heard of a god called Ock?' Chrestomanci coughed. 'He came to talk to me when you should have been the age you are now. He was worried – ' He coughed again. 'I shall have to save the rest of my breath for Heaven.'

They climbed on, and the stars swam around them, until the stuff they were climbing changed and became solider. Soon they were climbing a dark ramp, which flushed pearly as they went upwards. Here, Chrestomanci let go of Thasper's arm and blew his nose on a gold-edged handkerchief, with an air of relief. The pearl of the ramp grew to silver and the silver to dazzling white. At length, they were walking on level whiteness, through hall after hall after hall.

The gods were gathered to meet them. None of them looked cordial.

'I fear we are not properly dressed,' Chrestomanci murmured.

Thasper looked at the gods, and then at Chrestomanci, and squirmed with embarrassment. Fanciful and queer as Chrestomanci's garb was, it was still most obviously nightwear. The things on his feet were fur bedroom slippers. And there, looking like a piece of blue string around Chrestomanci's waist, was the turban Thasper should have been wearing. The gods were magnificent, in golden trousers and jewelled turbans, and got more so as they approached the greater gods. Thasper's eye was caught by a god in shining cloth of gold, who surprised him by beaming a friendly, almost anxious look at him. Opposite him was a huge liquid-looking figure draped in pearls and diamonds. This god swiftly, but quite definitely, winked. Thasper was too awed to react, but Chrestomanci calmly winked back.

At the end of the halls, upon a massive throne, towered the mighty figure of Great Zond, clothed in white and purple, with a crown on his head. Chrestomanci looked up at Zond and thoughtfully blew his nose. It was hardly respectful.

'For what reason do two mortals trespass in our halls?' Zond thundered coldly.

Chrestomanci sneezed. 'Because of your own folly,' he said. 'You gods of Theare have had everything so well worked out for so long that you can't see beyond your own routine.'

'I shall blast you for that,' Zond announced.

'Not if none of you wish to survive,' Chrestomanci said.

There was a long murmur of protest from the other gods. They wished to survive. They were trying to work out what Chrestomanci meant. Zond saw it as a threat to his authority and thought he had better be cautious. 'Proceed,' he said.

'One of your most efficient features,' Chrestomanci said, 'is that your prophecies always come true. So why, when a prophecy is unpleasant to you, do you think you can alter it? That, my good gods, is rank folly. Besides, no one can halt his own Dissolution, least of all you gods of Theare. But you forgot. You forgot you had deprived both yourselves and mankind of any kind of free will, by organizing yourselves so precisely. You pushed Thasper, the Sage of Dissolution, into my world, forgetting that there is still chance in my world. By chance, Thasper was discovered after only seven years. Lucky for Theare that he was. I shudder to think what might have happened if Thasper had remained three years old for all his allotted lifetime.'

'That was my fault!' cried Imperion. 'I take the

blame.' He turned to Thasper. 'Forgive me,' he said. 'You are my own son.'

Was this, Thasper wondered, what Alina meant by the gods blessing her womb? He had not thought it was more than a figure of speech. He looked at Imperion, blinking a little in the god's dazzle. He was not wholly impressed. A fine god, and an honest one, but Thasper could see he had a limited outlook. 'Of course I forgive you,' he said politely.

'It is also lucky,' Chrestomanci said, 'that none of you succeeded in killing the Sage. Thasper is a god's son. That means there can only ever be one of him, and because of your prophecy he has to be alive to preach Dissolution. You could have destroyed Theare. As it is, you have caused it to blur into a mass of cracks. Theare is too well organized to divide into two alternative worlds, like my world would. Instead, events have had to happen which could not have happened. Theare has cracked and warped, and you have all but brought about your own Dissolution.'

'What can we do?' Zond said, aghast.

'There's only one thing you can do,' Chrestomanci told him. 'Let Thasper be. Let him preach Dissolution and stop trying to blow him up. That will bring about free will and a free future. Then either Theare will heal, or it will split, cleanly and painlessly, into two healthy new worlds.'

'So we bring about our own downfall?' Zond asked mournfully.

'It was always inevitable,' said Chrestomanci.

Zond sighed. 'Very well. Thasper, son of Imperion, I reluctantly give you my blessing to go forth and preach Dissolution. Go in peace.'

Thasper bowed. Then he stood there silent a long time. He did not notice Imperion and Ock both trying to attract his attention. The newspaper report had talked of the Sage as full of anguish and self-doubt. Now he knew why. He looked at Chrestomanci, who was blowing his nose again. 'How can I preach Dissolution?' he said. 'How can I not believe in the gods when I have seen them for myself?'

'That's a question you certainly should be asking,' Chrestomanci croaked. 'Go down to Theare and ask it.' Thasper nodded and turned to go. Chrestomanci leaned towards him and said, from behind his handkerchief 'Ask yourself this too: Can the gods catch flu? I think I may have given it to all of them. Find out and let me know, there's a good chap.'